STORM

21 DESIGNS by Kim Hargreaves

CREDITS

DESIGNS & STYLING
Kim Hargreaves

EDITOR
Kathleen Hargreaves

MODEL
Angharad Hunt

HAIR & MAKE-UP
Diana Fisher

PHOTOGRAPHY & EDITORIAL DESIGN
Graham Watts

LAYOUTS
Angela Lin

PATTERNS
Sue Whiting & Tricia McKenzie

© Copyright Kim Hargreaves 2013.

First published in 2013 by Kim Hargreaves, Intake Cottage, 26 Underbank Old Road, Holmfirth, West Yorkshire, HD9 1EA, England.

All Rights Reserved.

No part of this book may be reproduced, stored in a retrieval system or transmitted in any form or by any means—electronic, electrostatic, magnetic tape, mechanical, photocopying, scanning, recording or otherwise—without prior permission in writing from the publisher.

British Library Cataloguing in Publication Data.
A catalogue record for this book is available from the British Library.

ISBN-10   1-906487-18-8
ISBN-13   978-1-906487-18-8

CONTENTS

7 THE DESIGNS
A collection of contrasts and attitude

58 THE PATTERNS
Find the information needed to complete the individual designs

98 INFORMATION
A guide to help with techniques and finishing touches

101 INDEX

STORM

A collection of contrasts and attitude, at first glance it appears slightly tough, slightly edgy, however look a little deeper and you'll find that the pieces are true classics and have a soft feminine side. In a story where delicate fabrics of satin and lace work alongside boyish plaid and sturdy biker boots, expect the unexpected

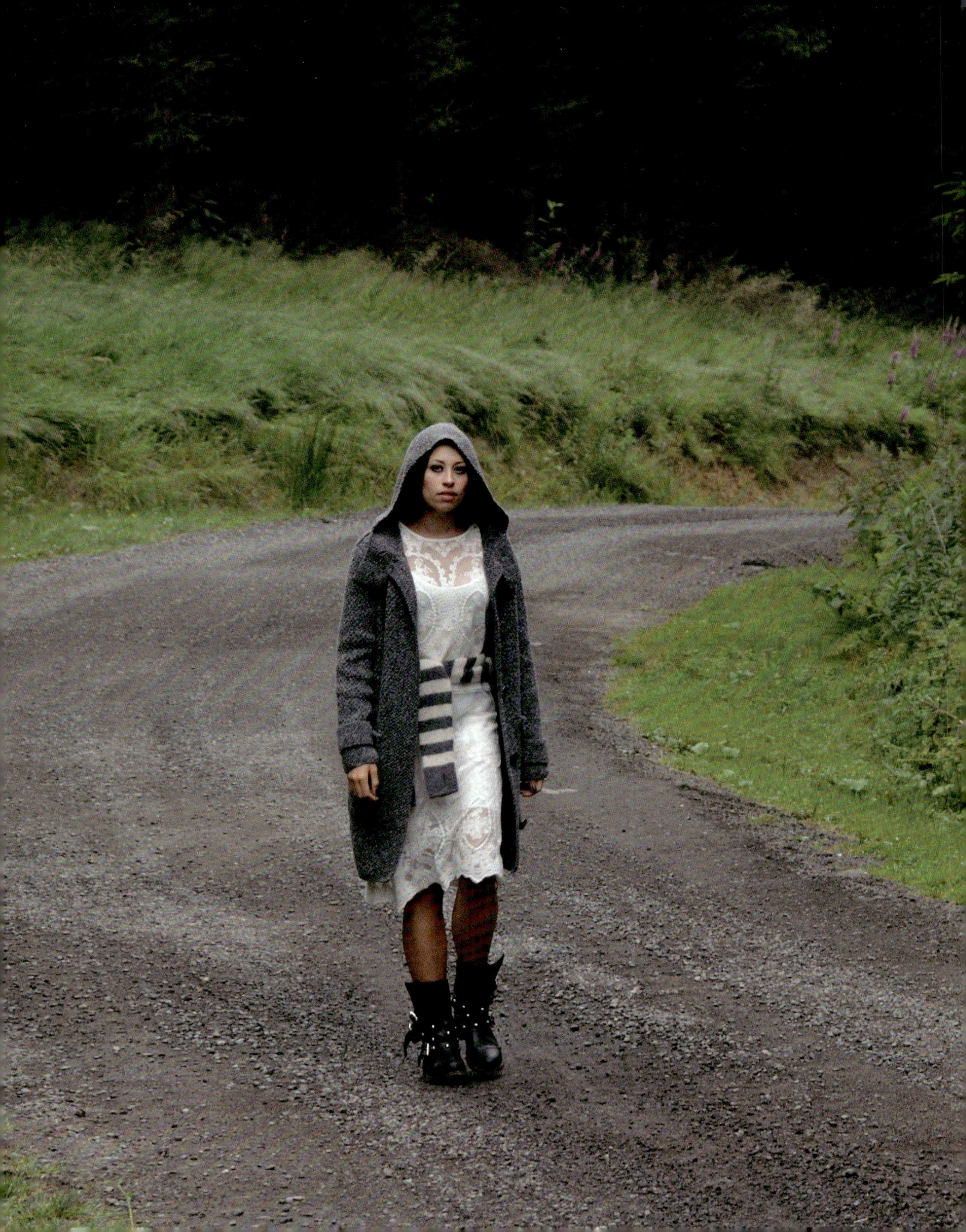

ECHO a tweed duffle coat with cosy hood, tops a vintage dress and **CARIS** sweater, just seen

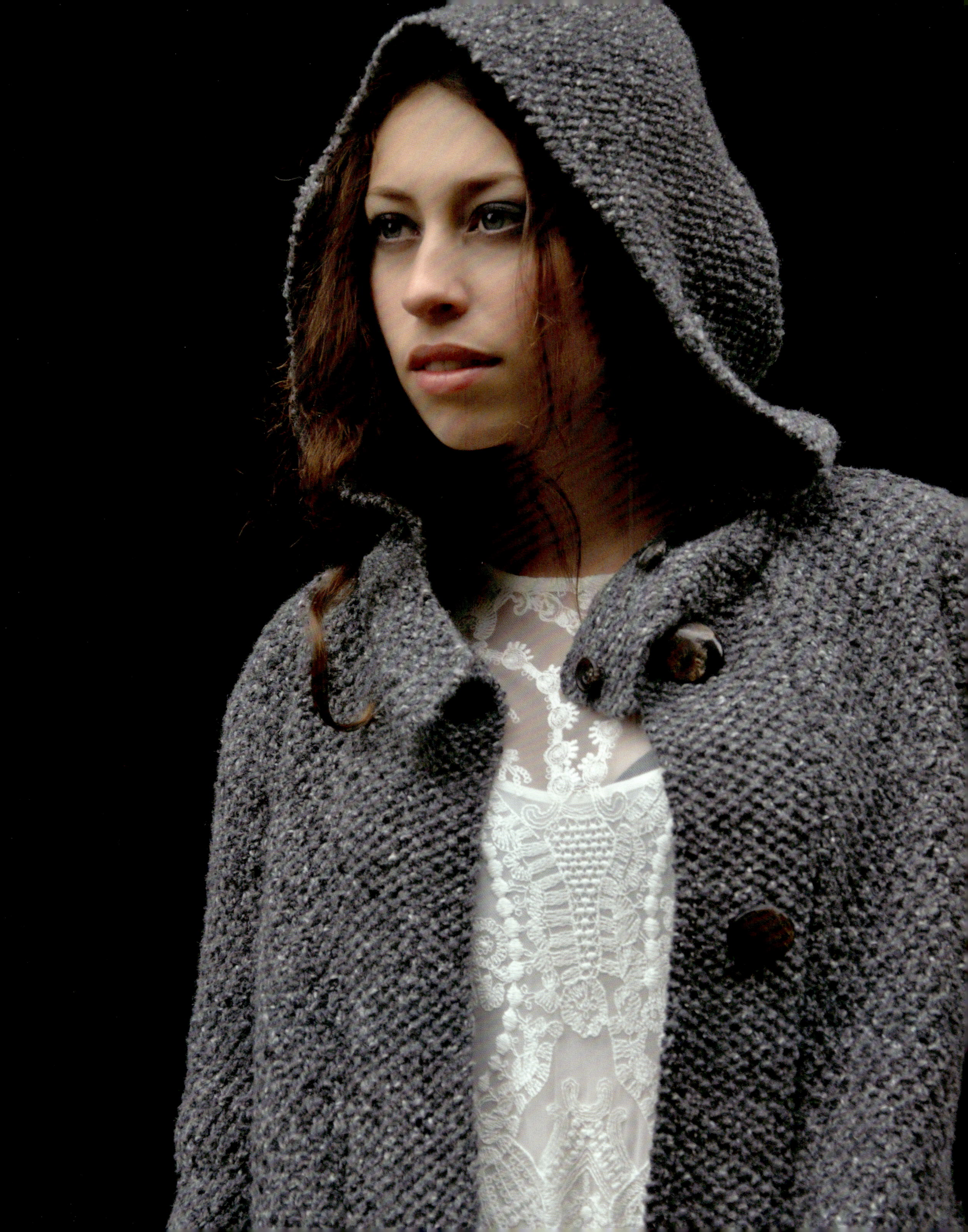

SHALE a neat tailored blazer worn with beaded skirt and contrasting heavy belt

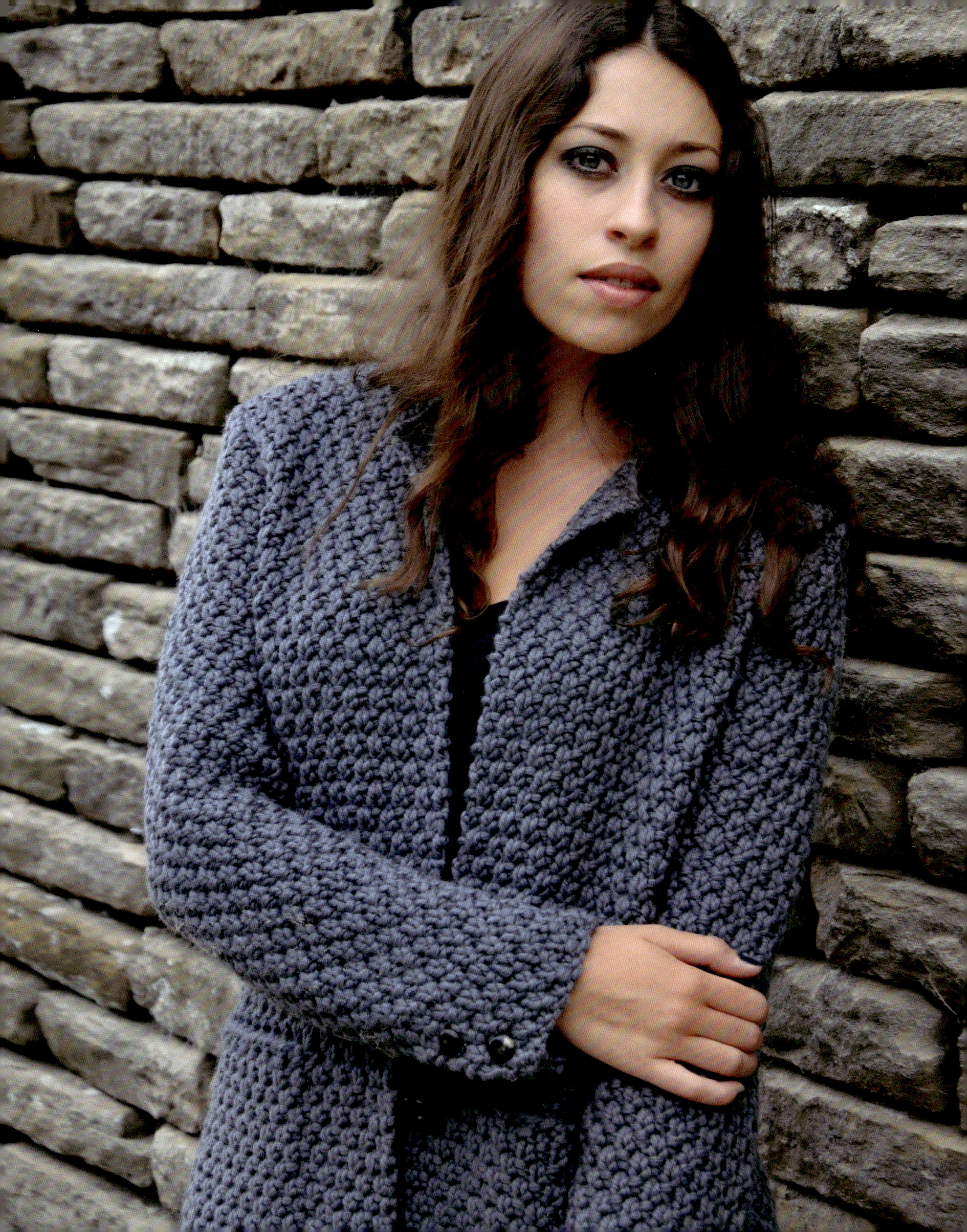

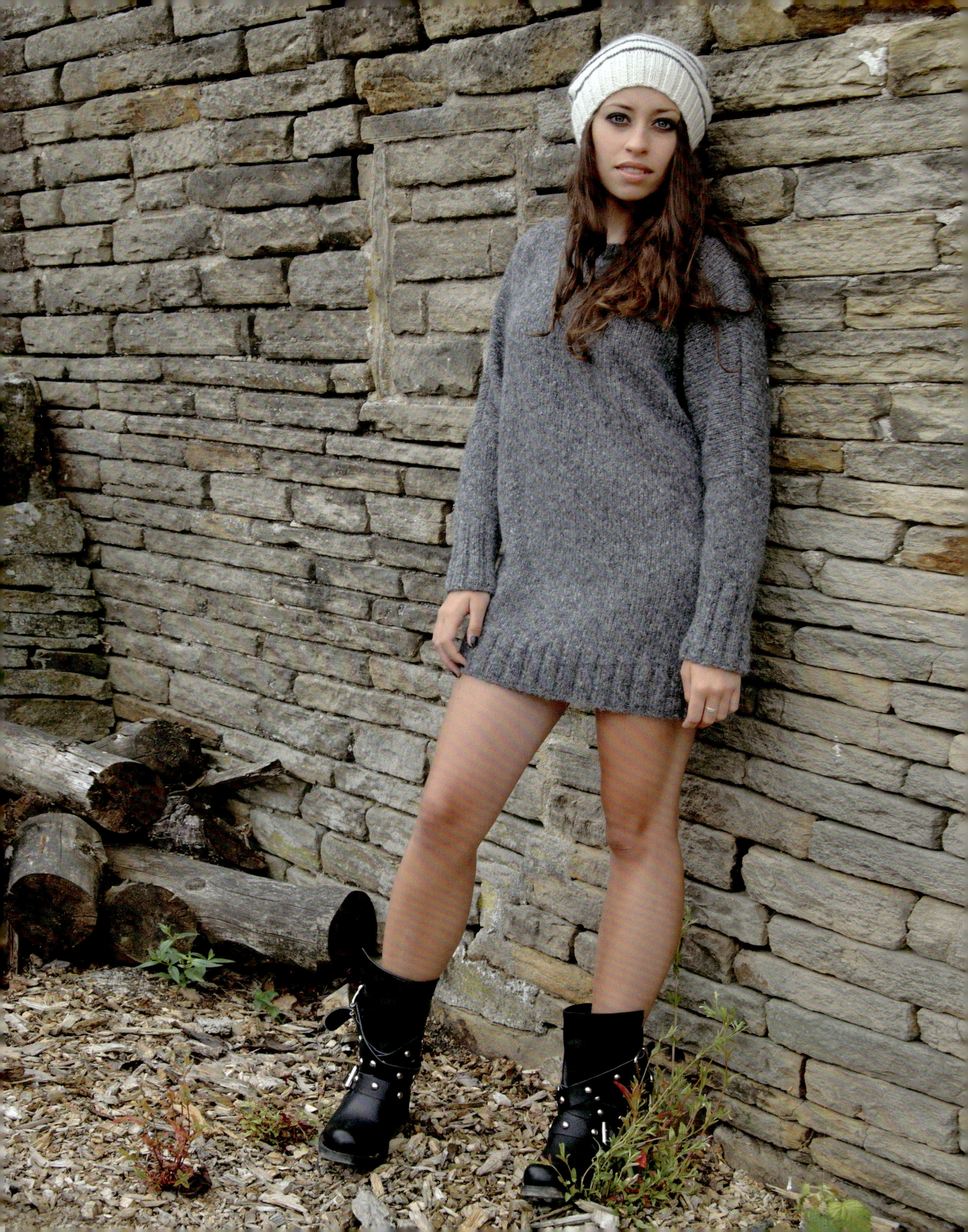

TEMPEST a soft mini dress worn simply with **SMOKY** a slouchy striped hat

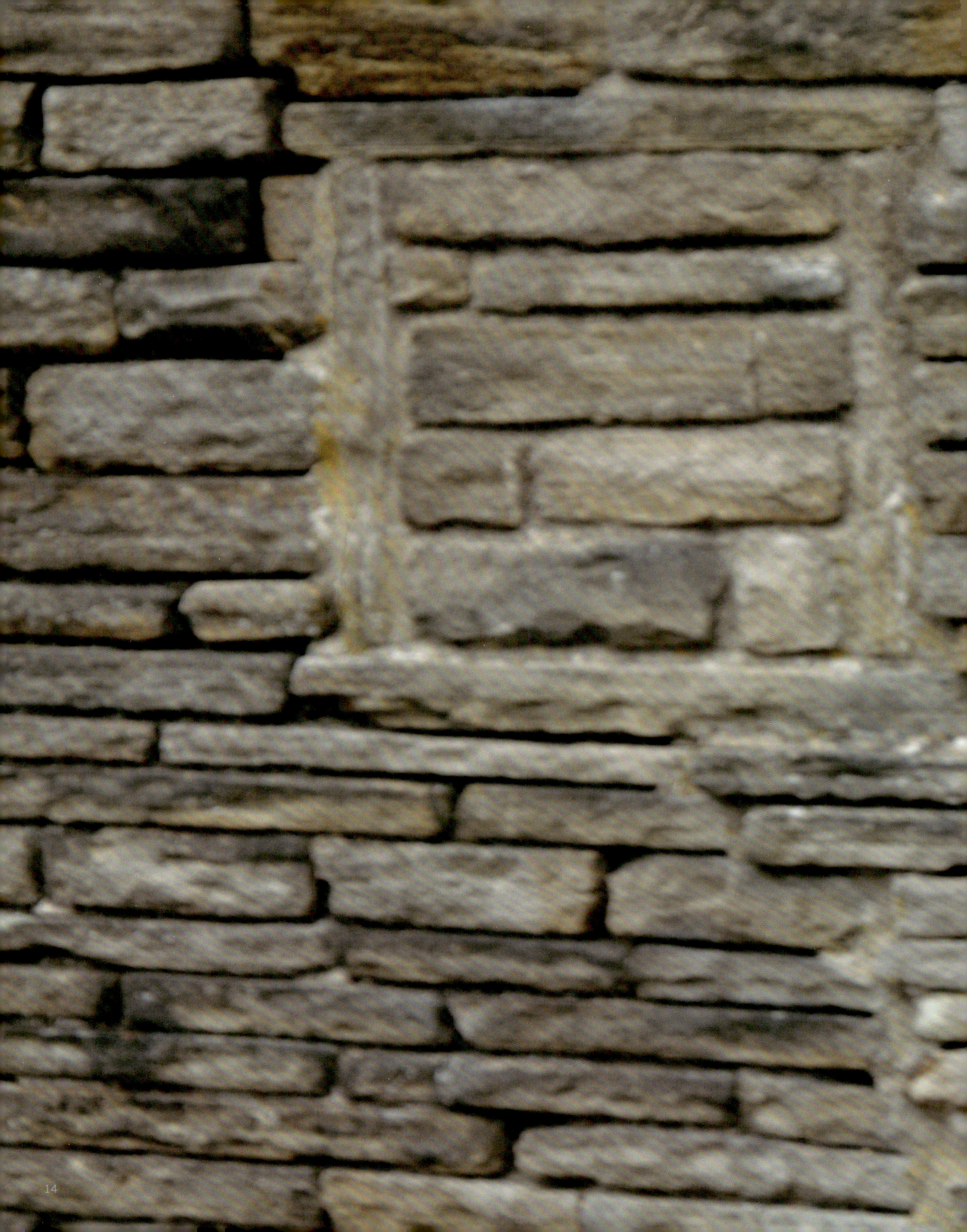

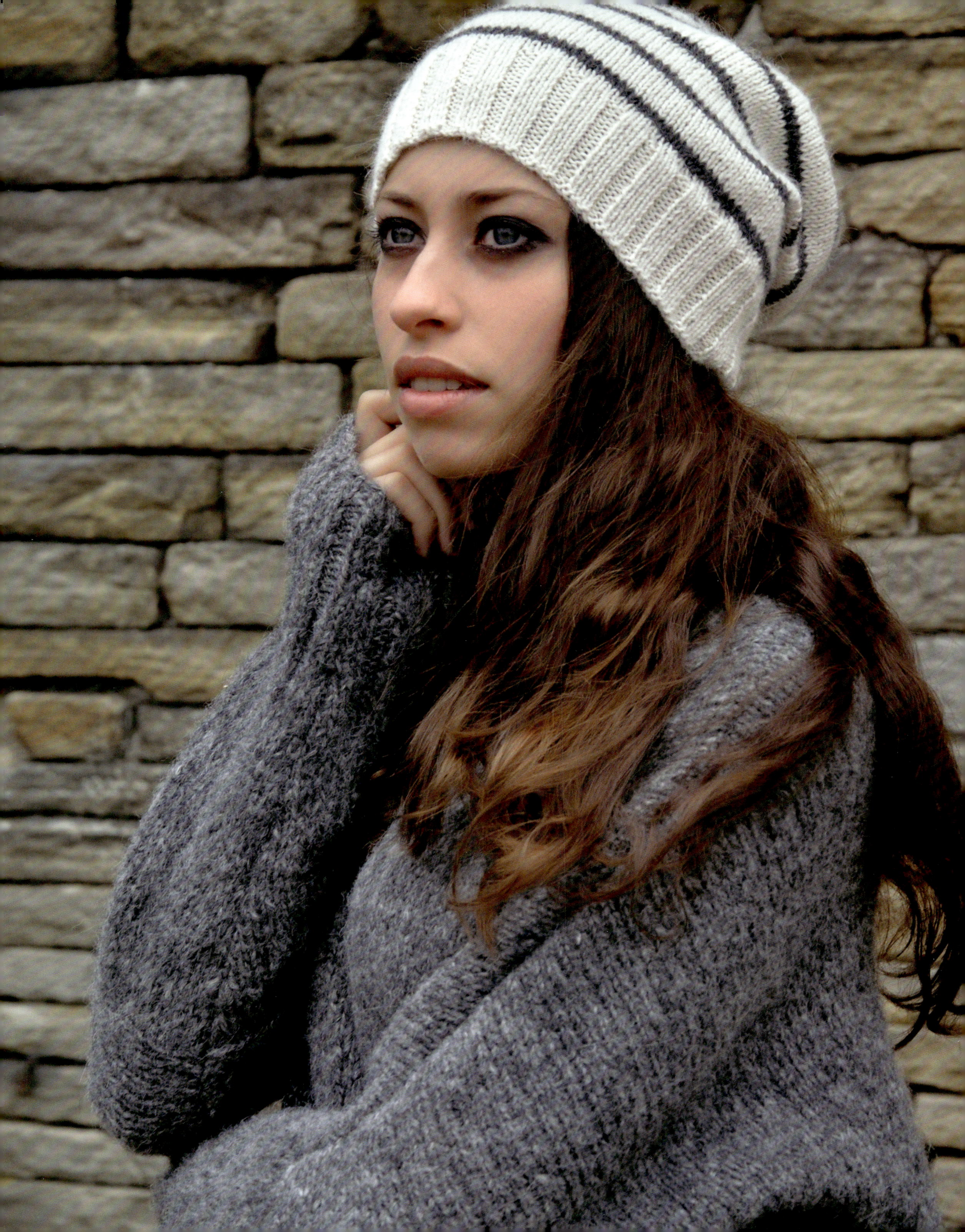

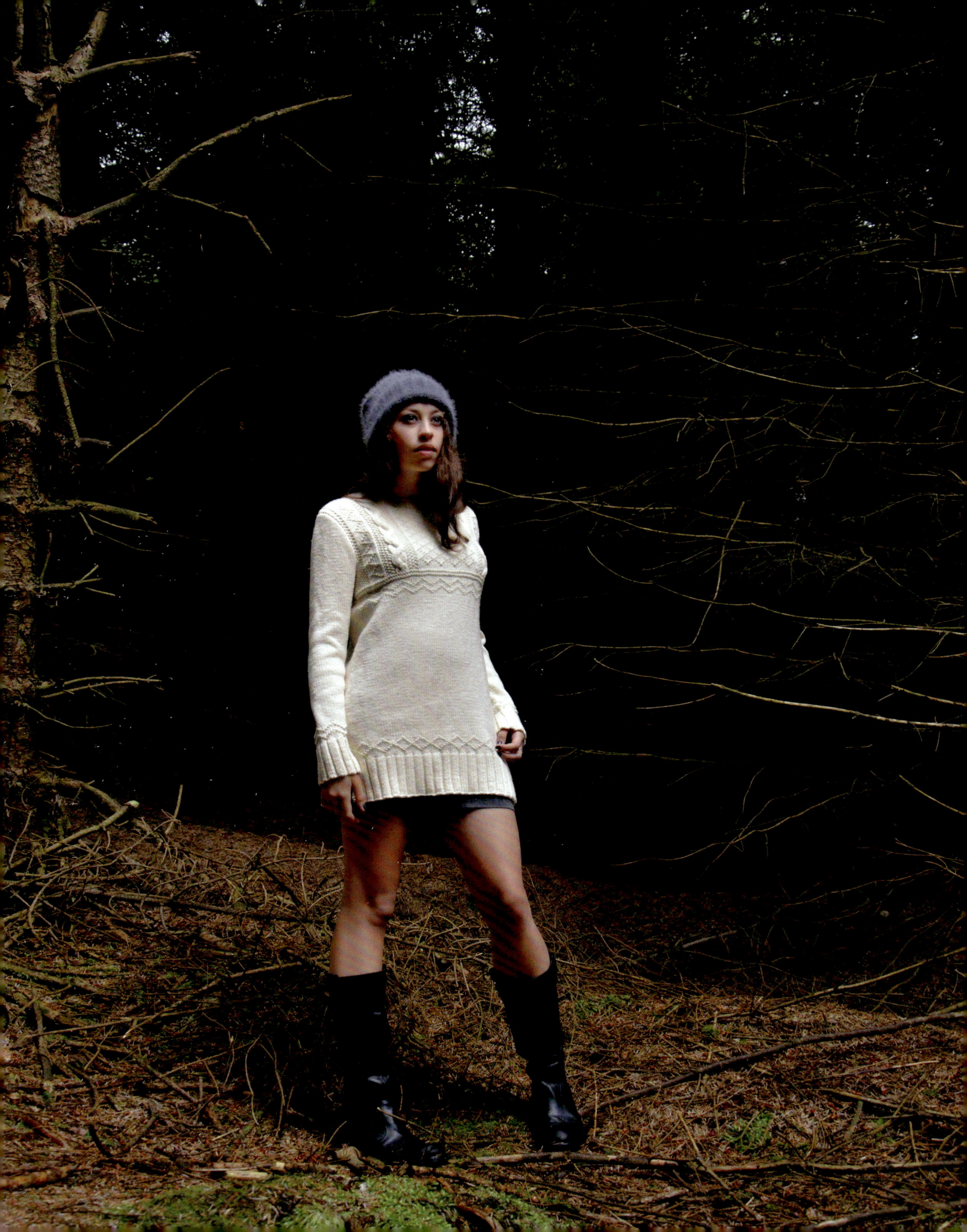

WEALD reworking a classic, an A-line guernsey style sweater — worn with **BRAM** a ribbed hat

ANNIS a pretty close-fitting sweater with button neckline worked in sumptuous angora

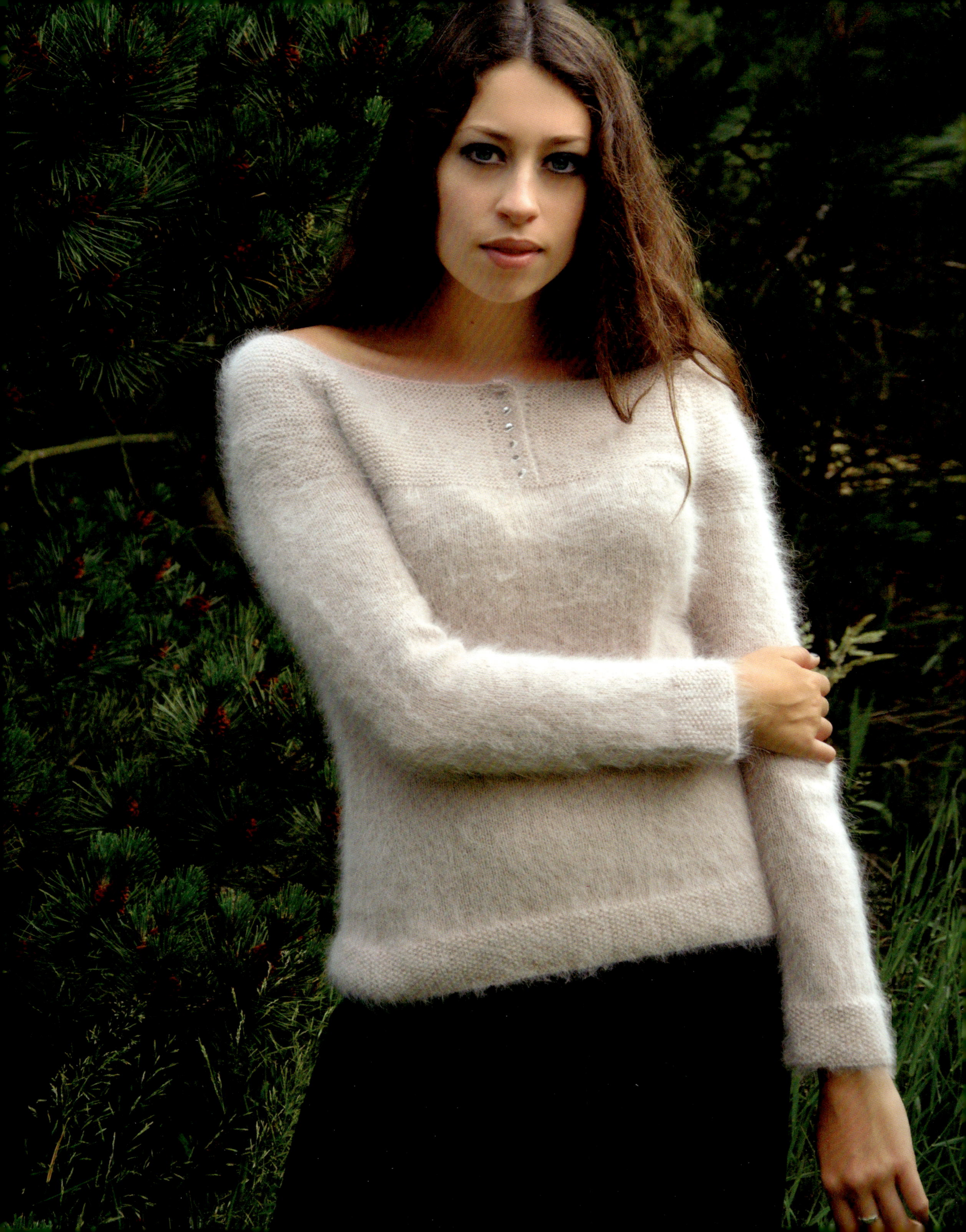

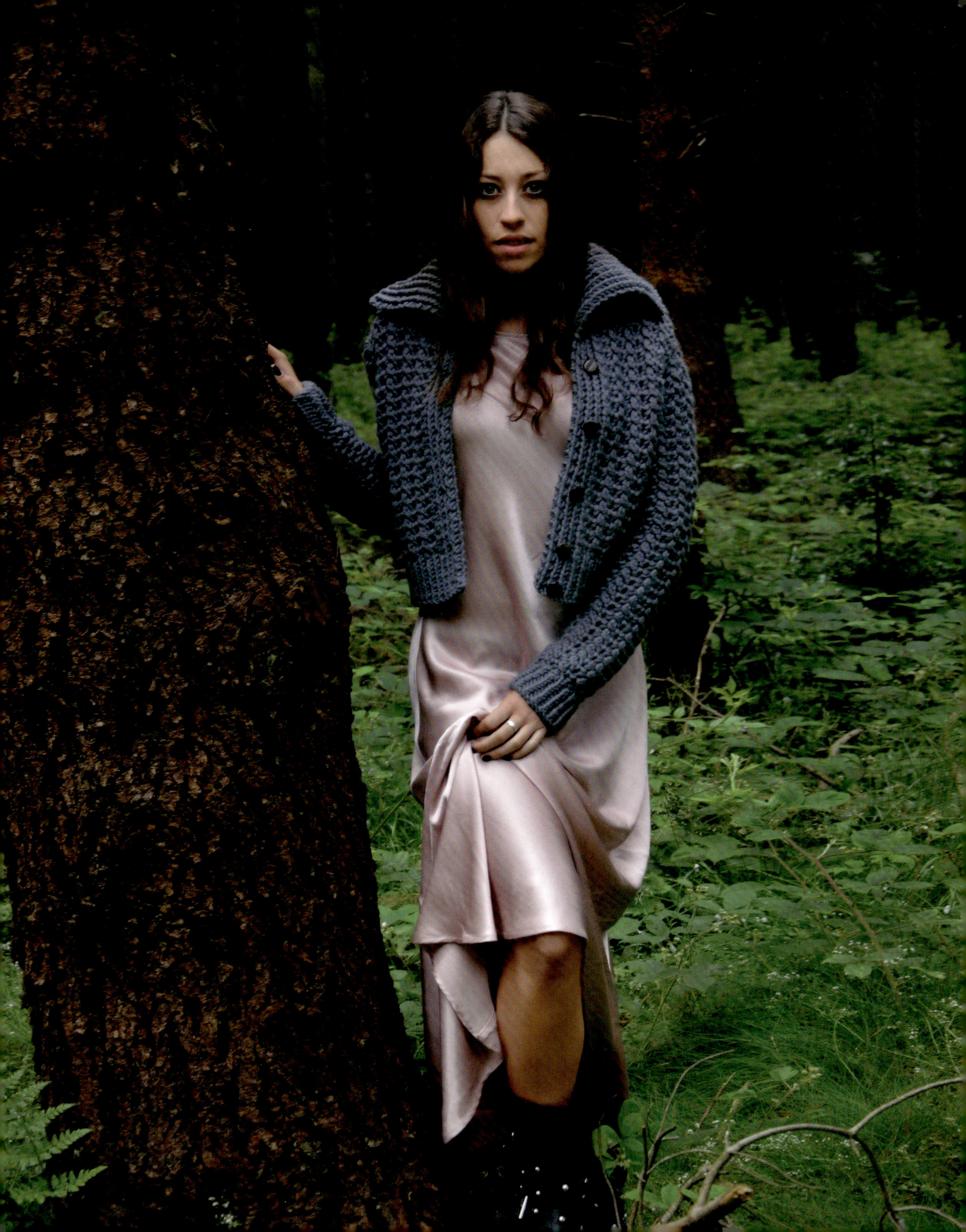

STOMP a textured boxy jacket with cosy collar worn over slinky satin

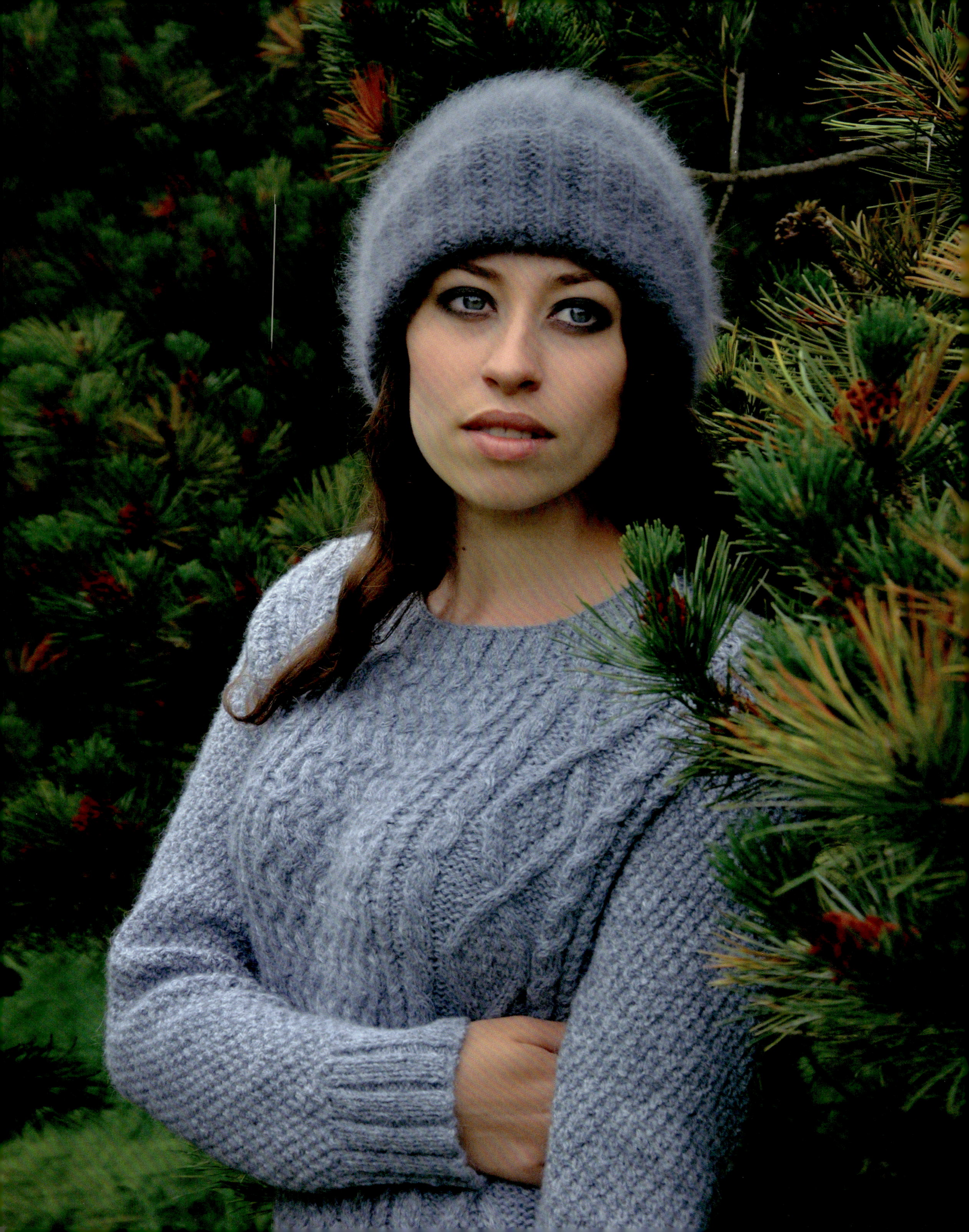

WILDA a fitted midi length aran dress worn with **BRAM** ribbed hat

THOR a classic fairisle boyfriend cardigan keeping it simple in monotone shades

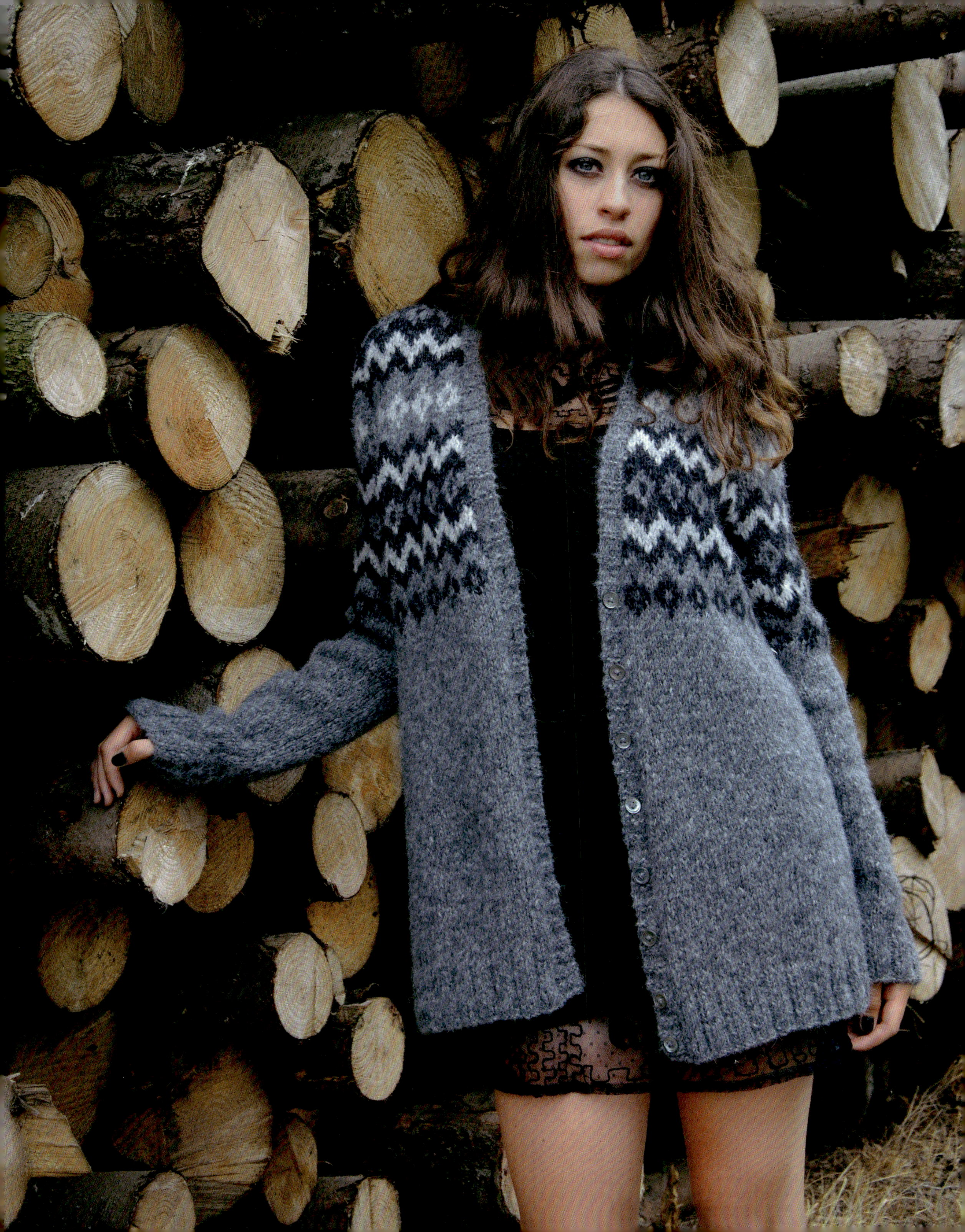

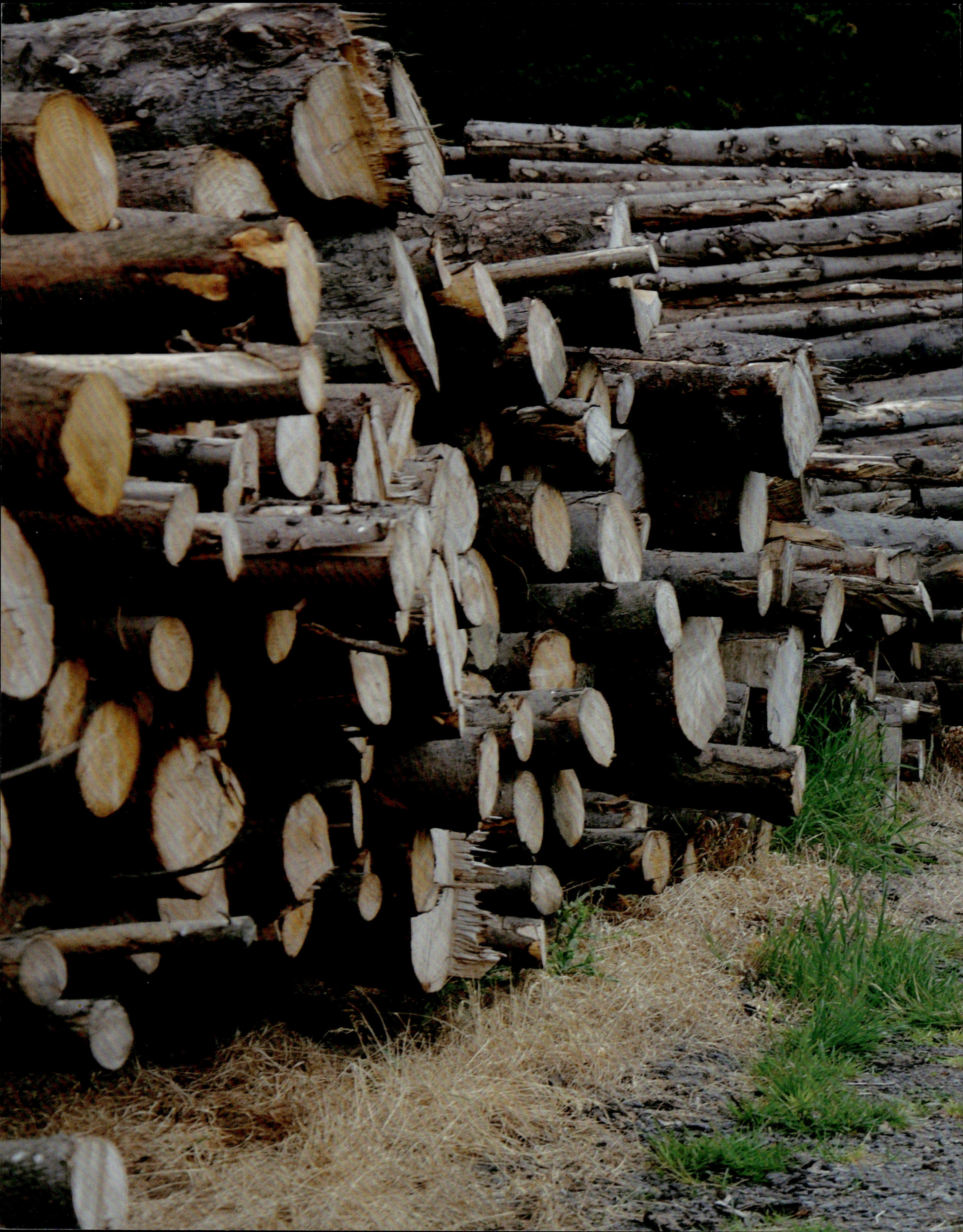

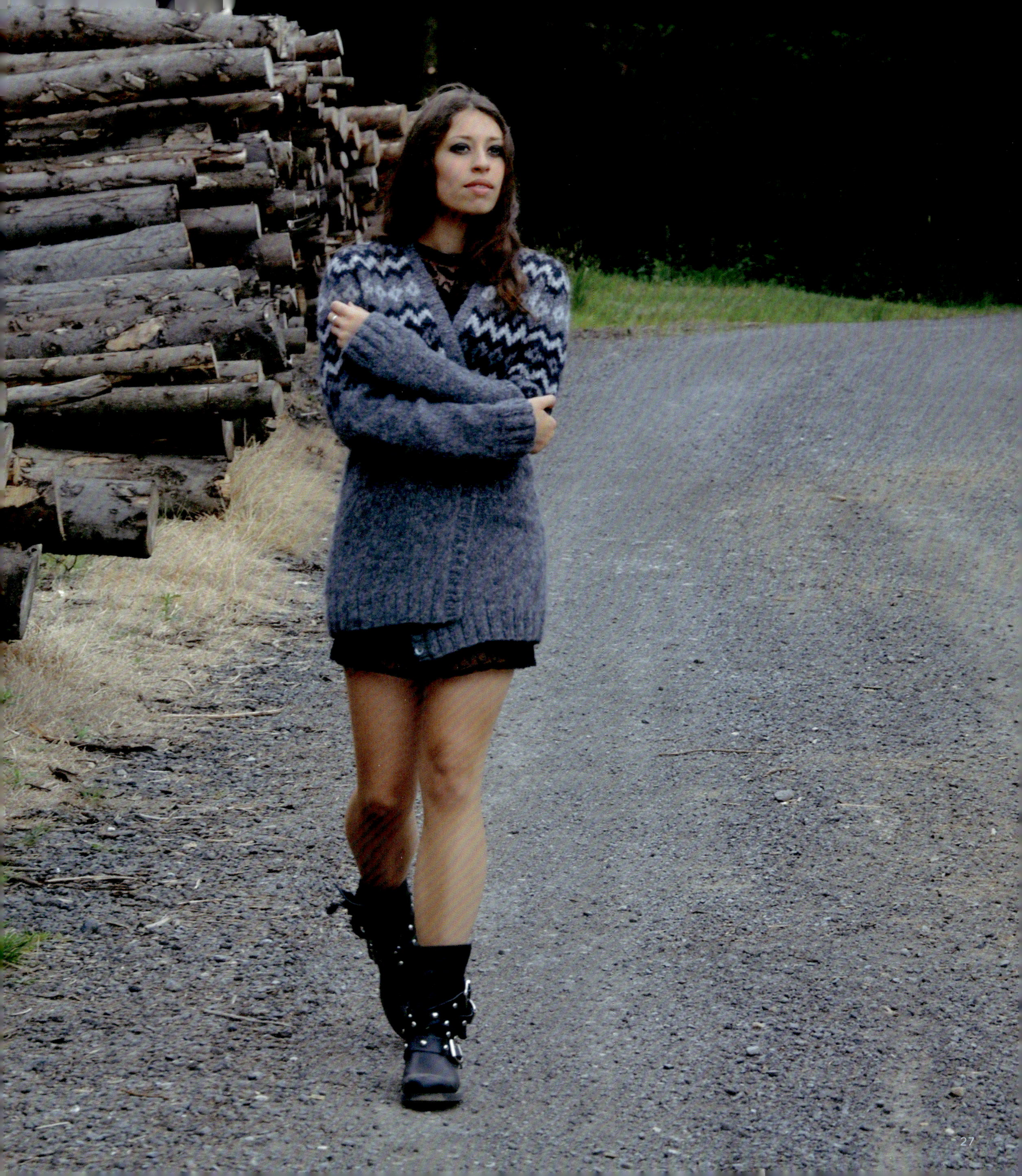

FARA a traditional button through sweater worn youthfully with plaid

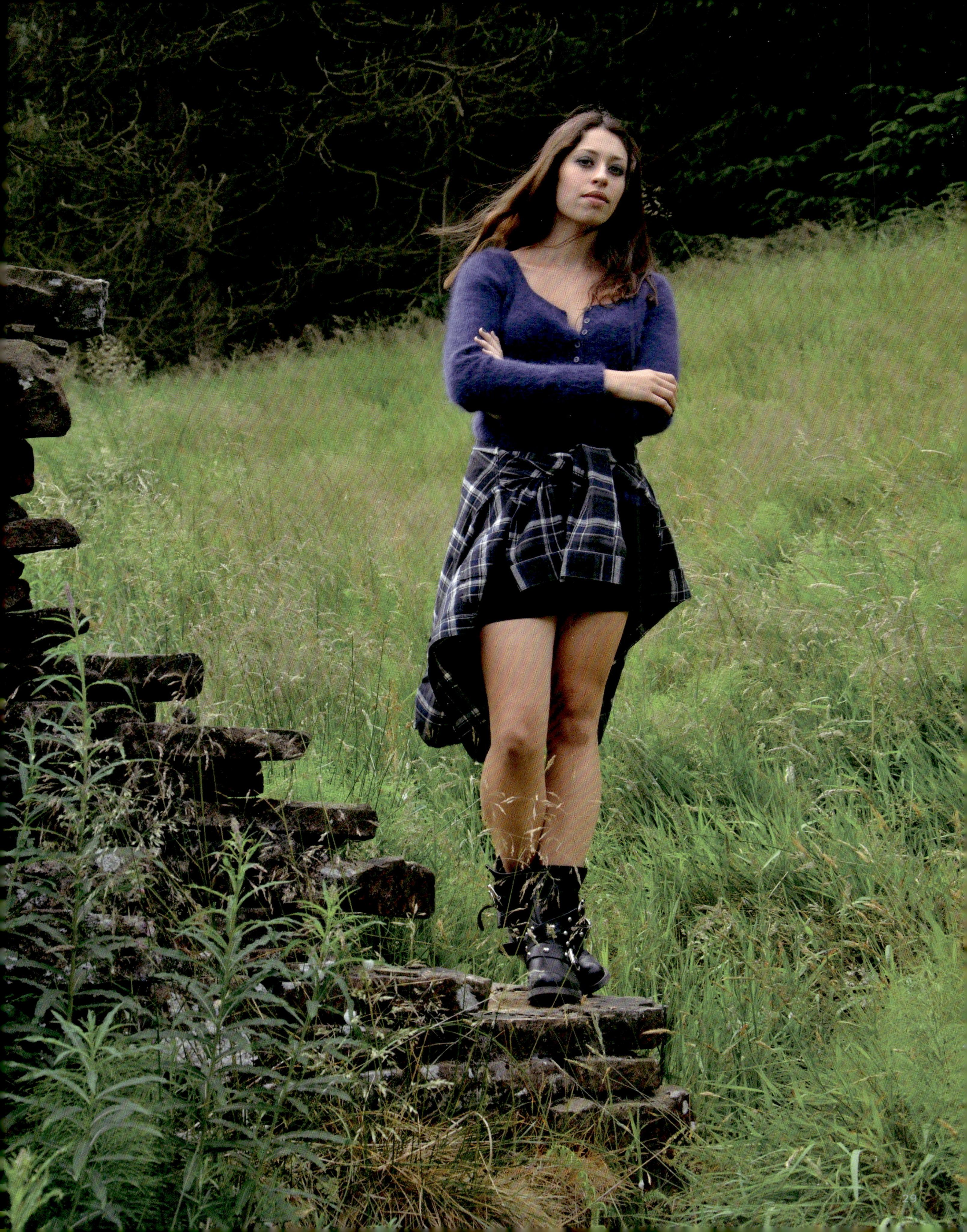

DREW a soft ribbed boyfriend cardigan worn with **BRAM** a slouchy hat

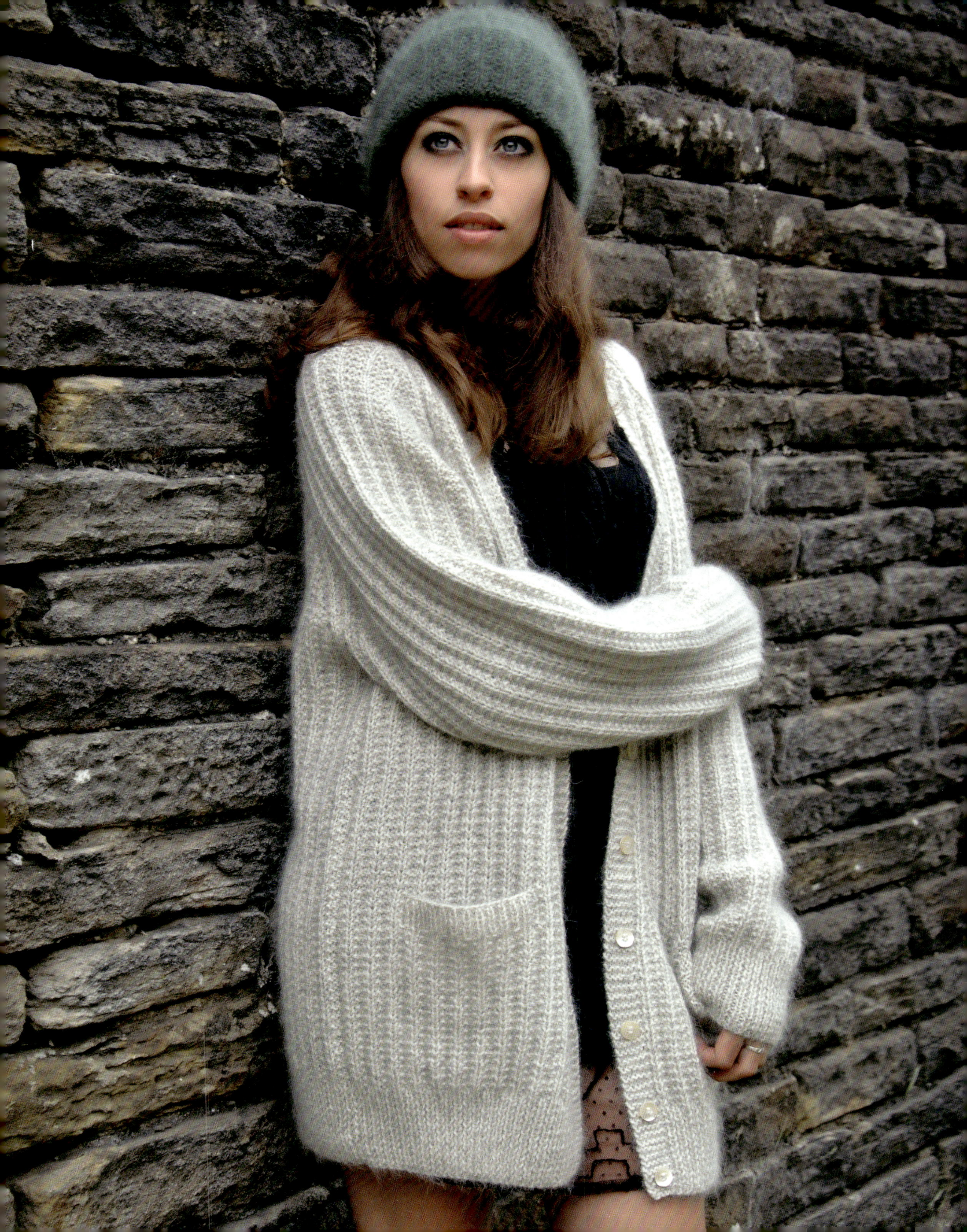

This page **BRAM** a cosy ribbed hat, opposite, **FOGGY** a long-line fairlise scarf in monotone shades

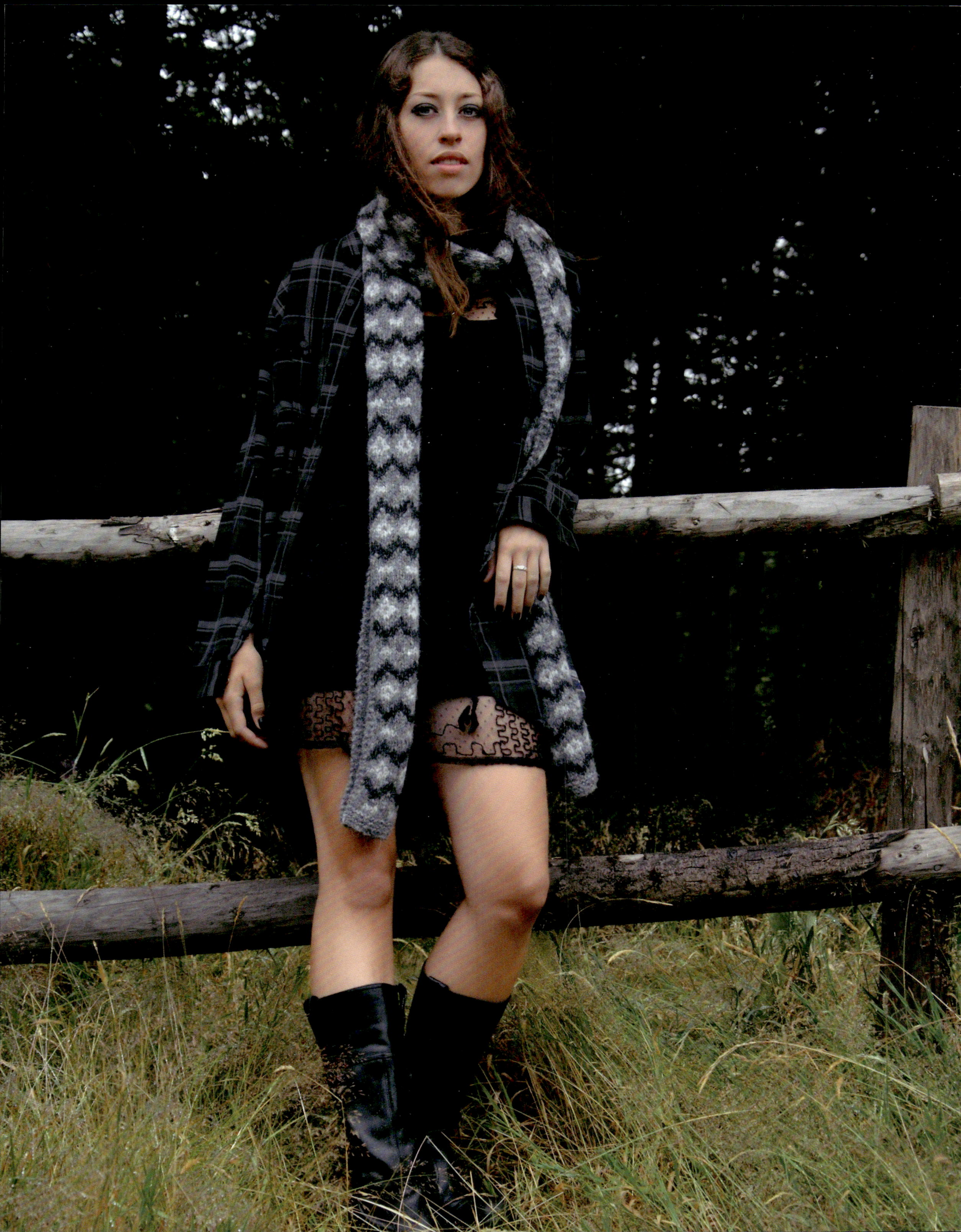

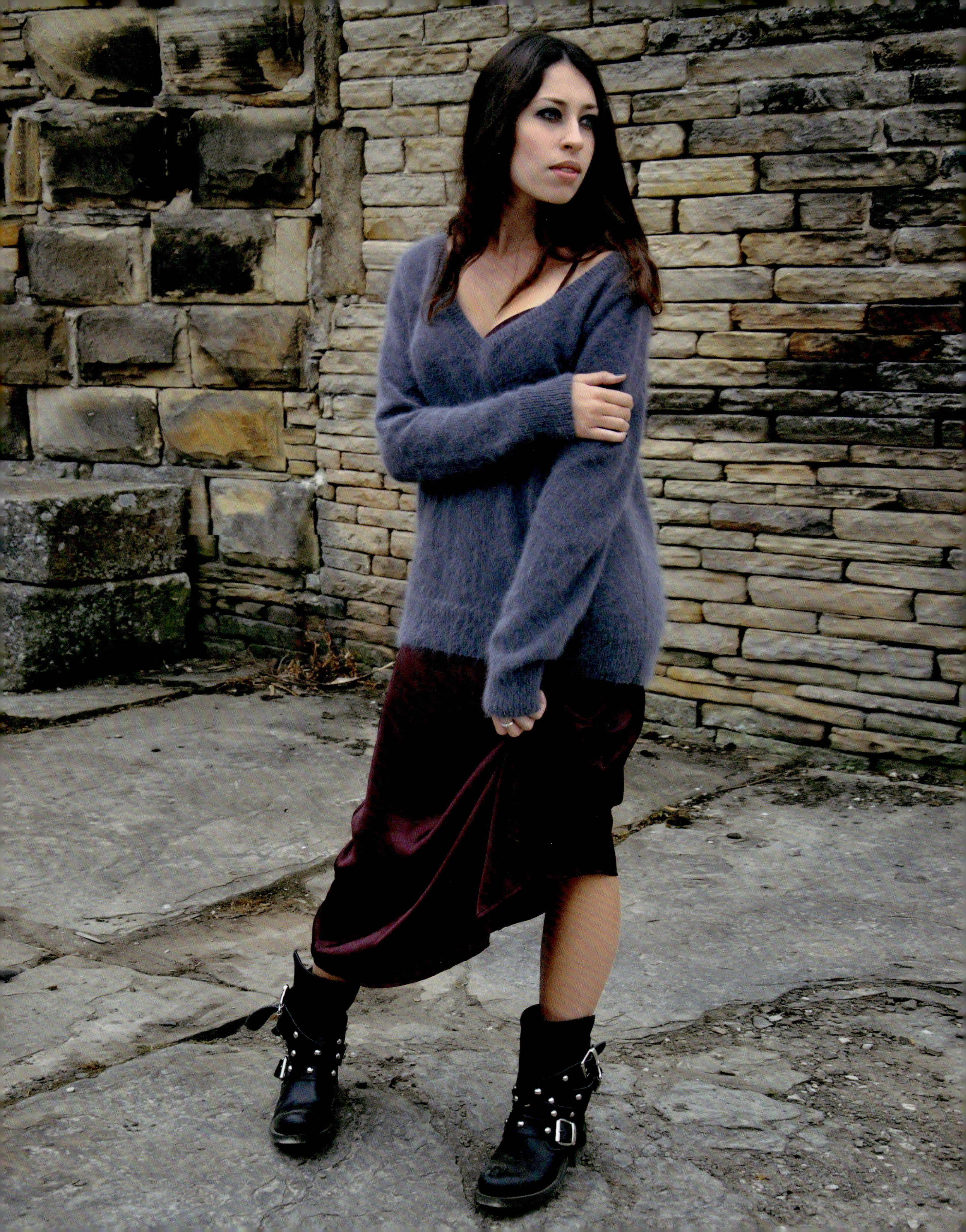

BLAIR a relaxed V-neck sweater worn with satin

ISOLDE an elegant ribbed wrap creates a dramatic look

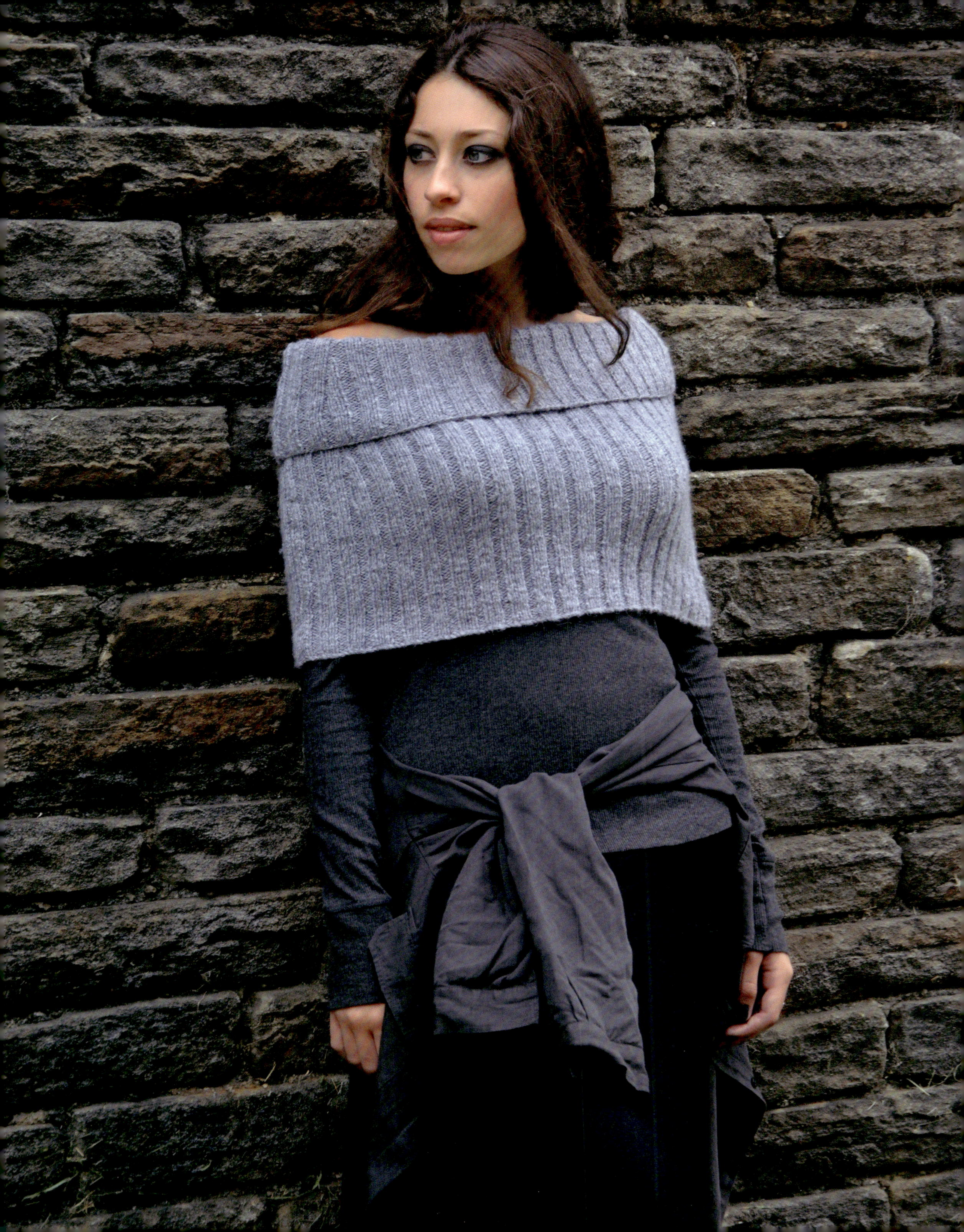

This page, **SMOKY** a slouchy striped hat, opposite, **MYRA** a neat cardigan worked in garter stitch with eyelet peplum

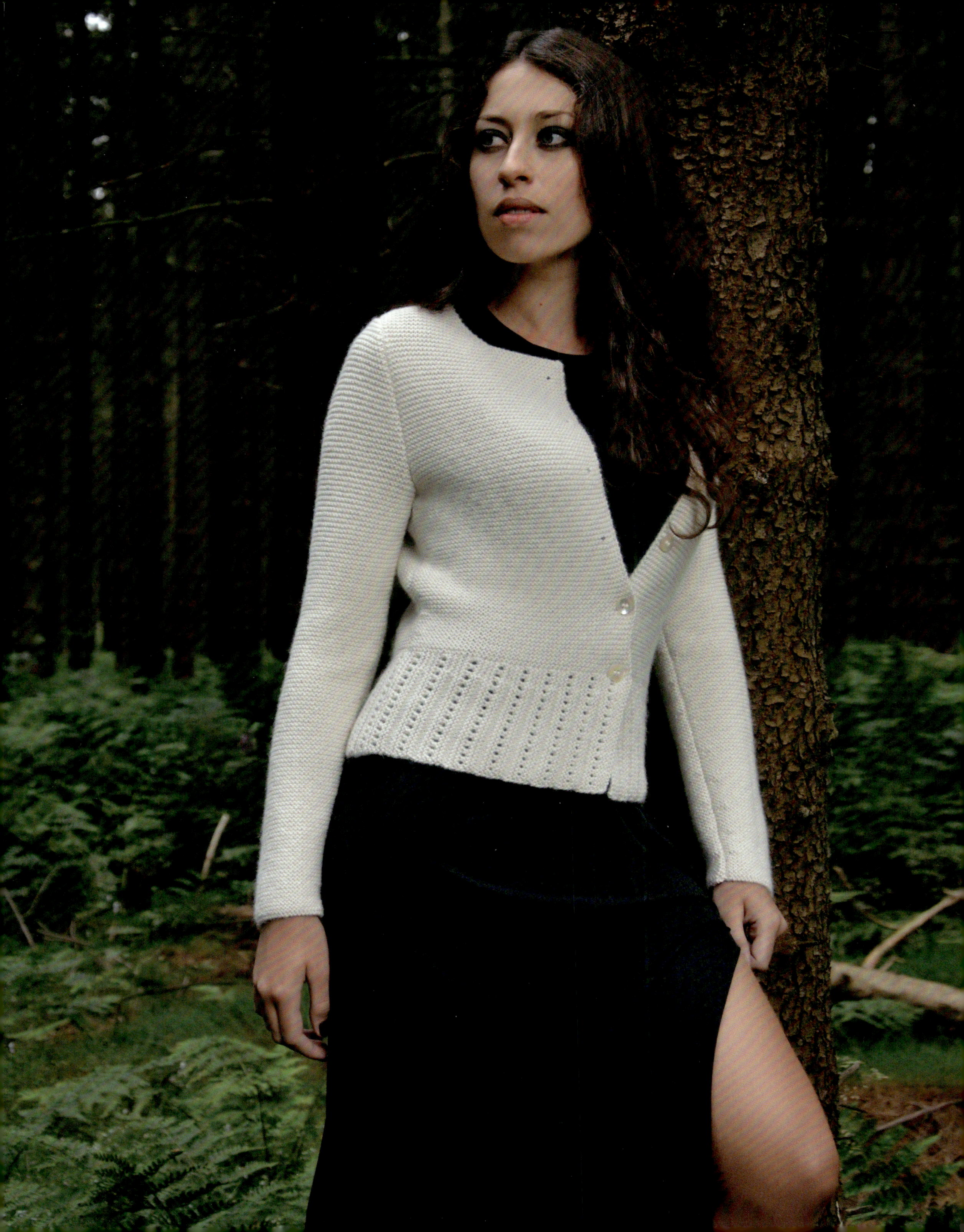

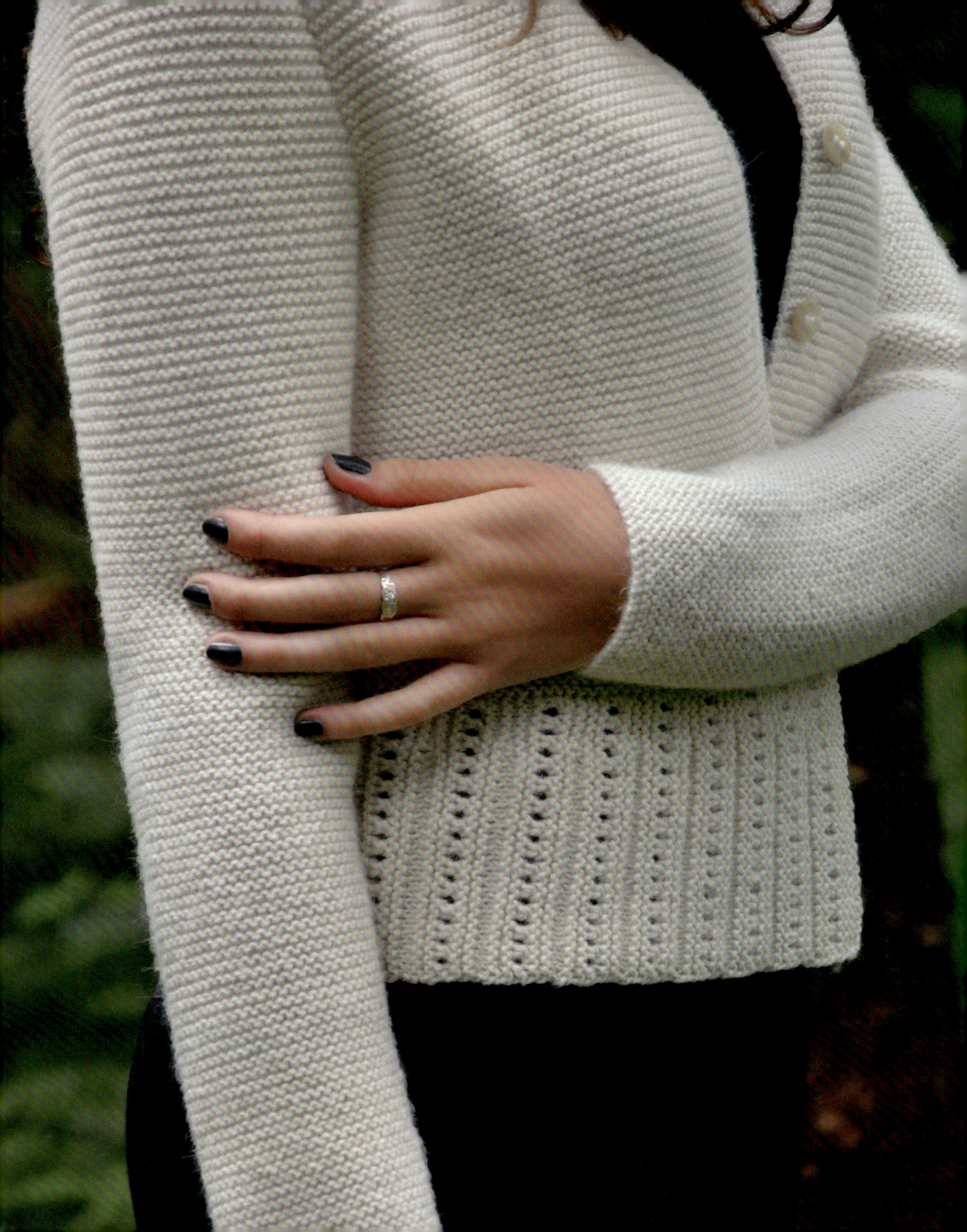

MYRA a pretty cardigan worked in garter stitch with eyelet peplum

TYNE playing with tradition, a fitted Guernsey style sweater

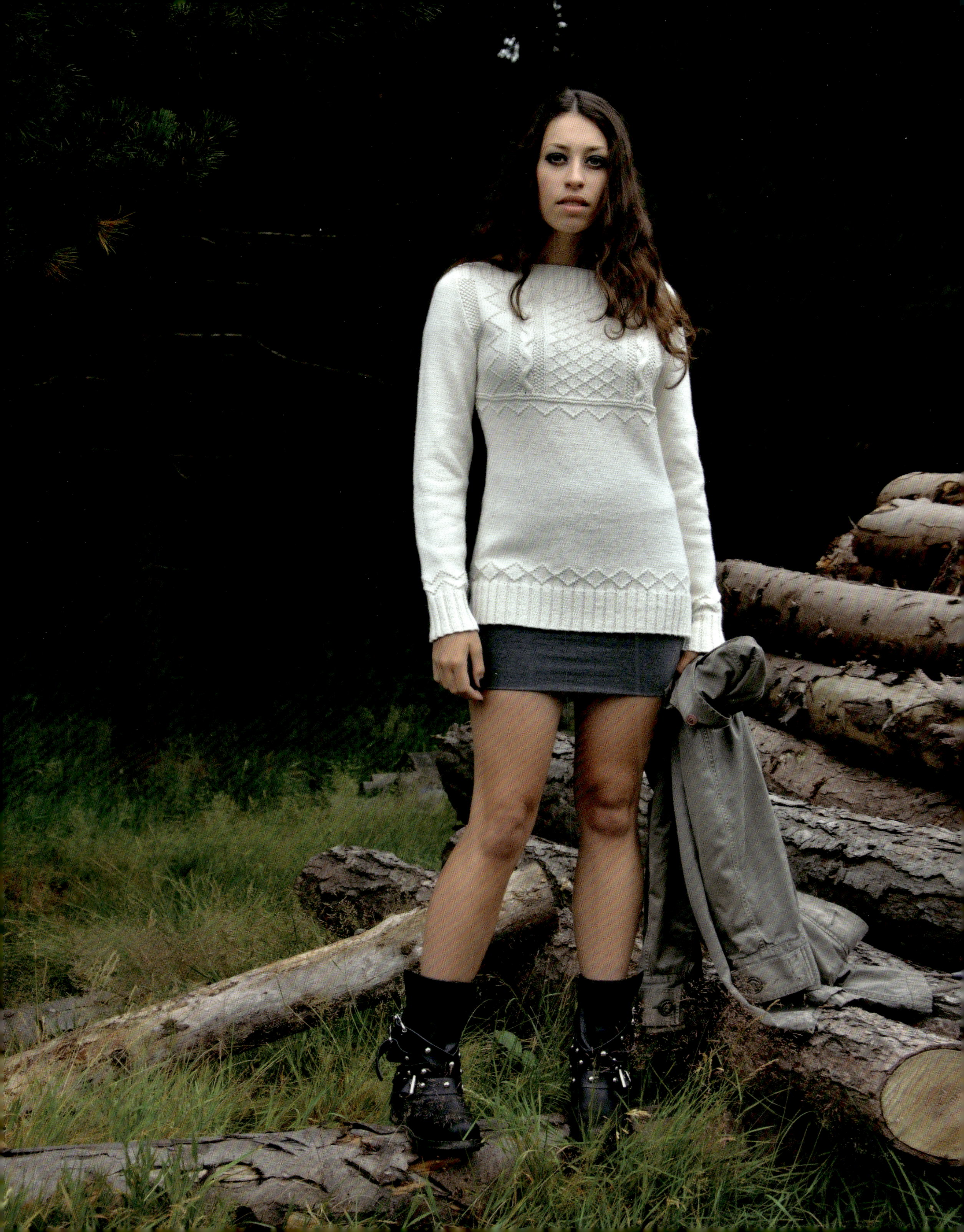

44

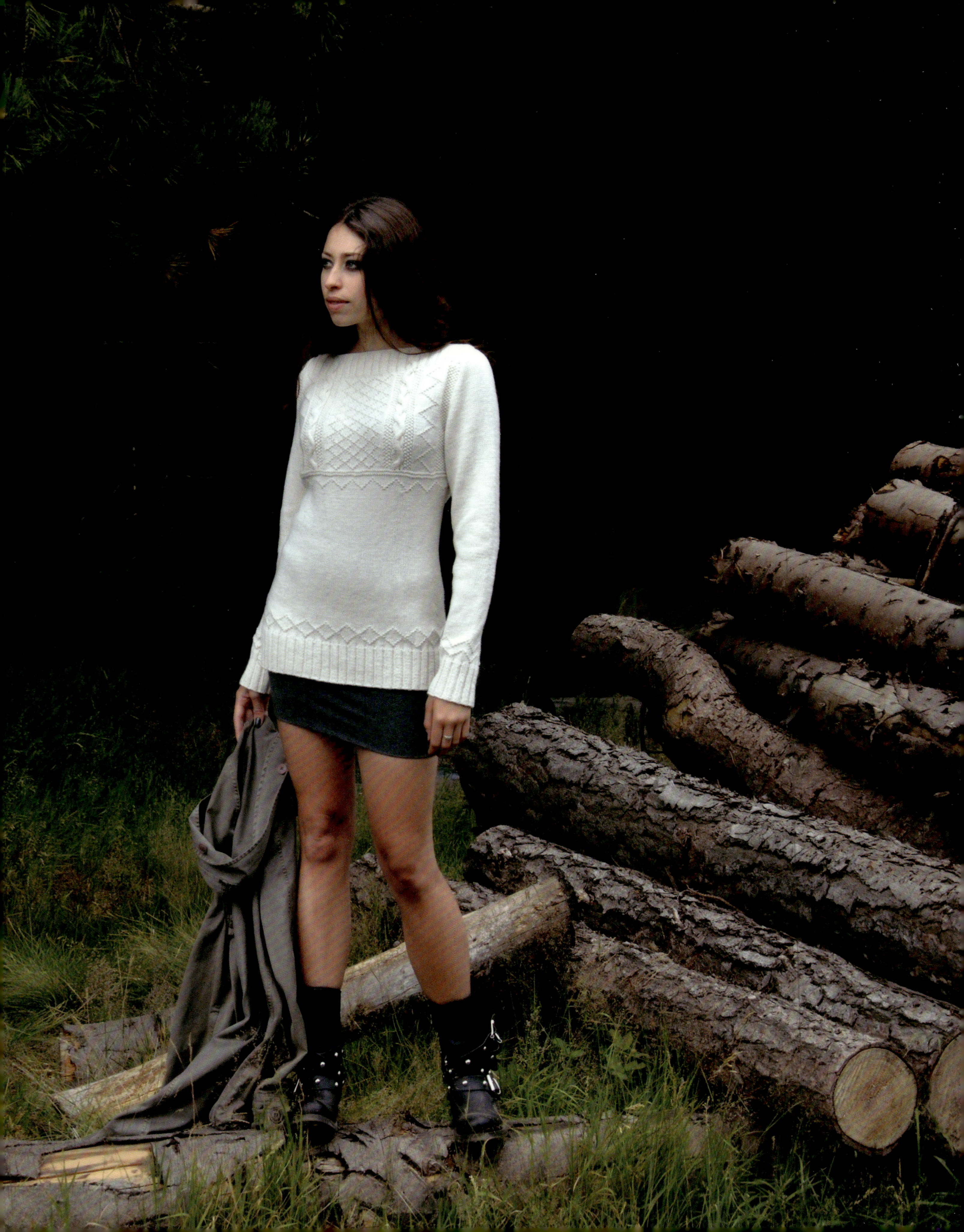

CARIS a close-fitting sweater set off by bold stripes

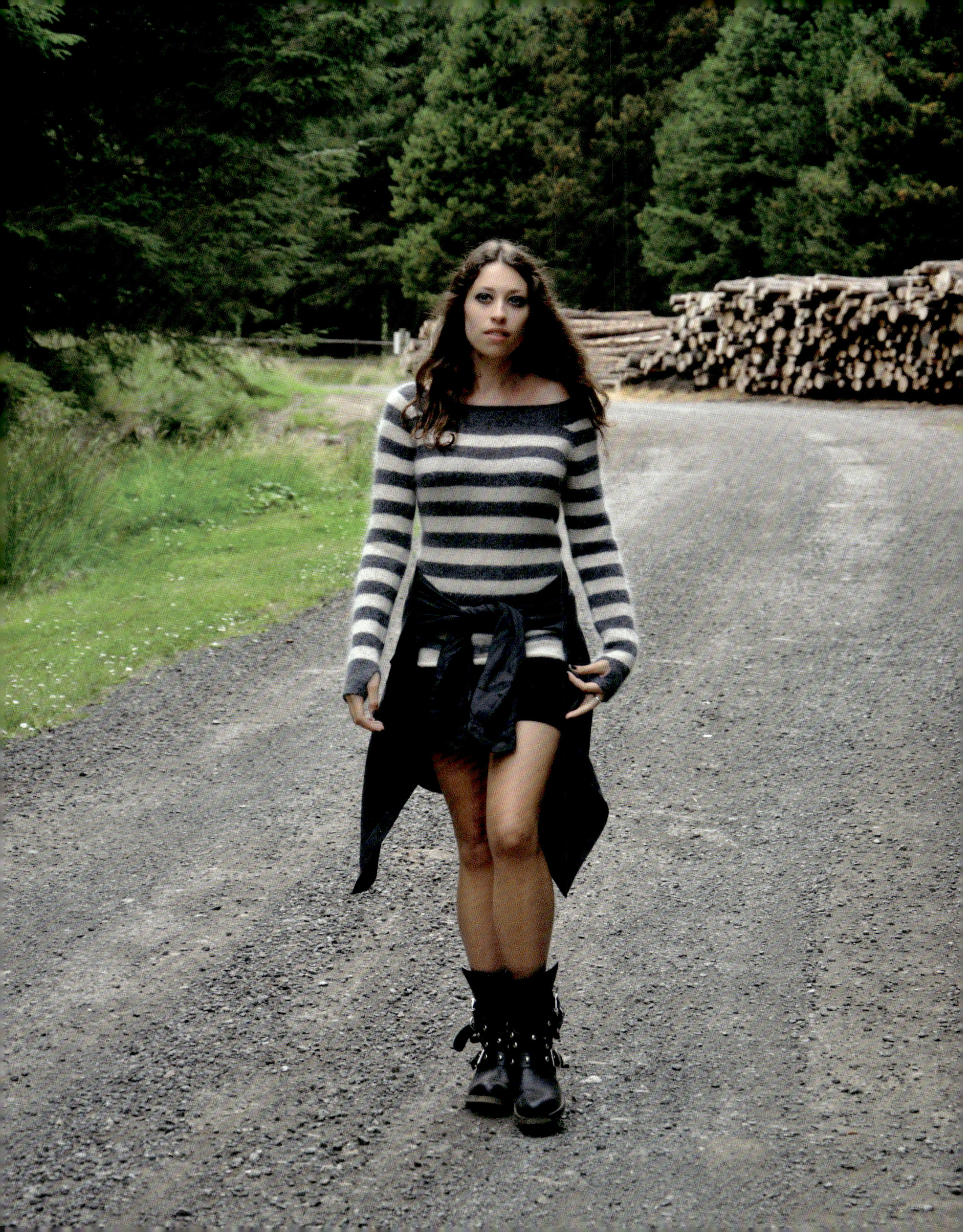

BRYN a sweater of timeless simplicity works well with a bit of sparkle

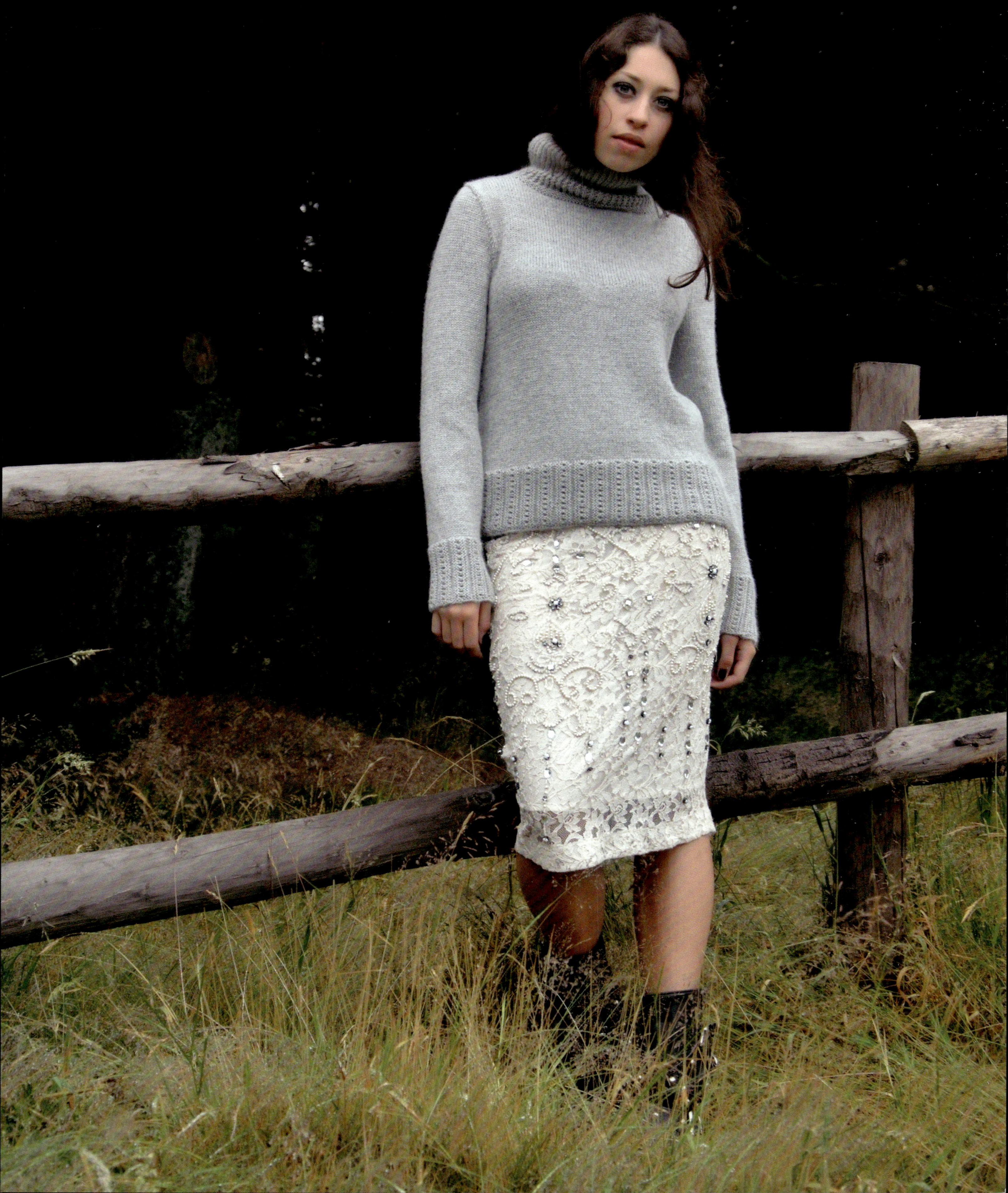

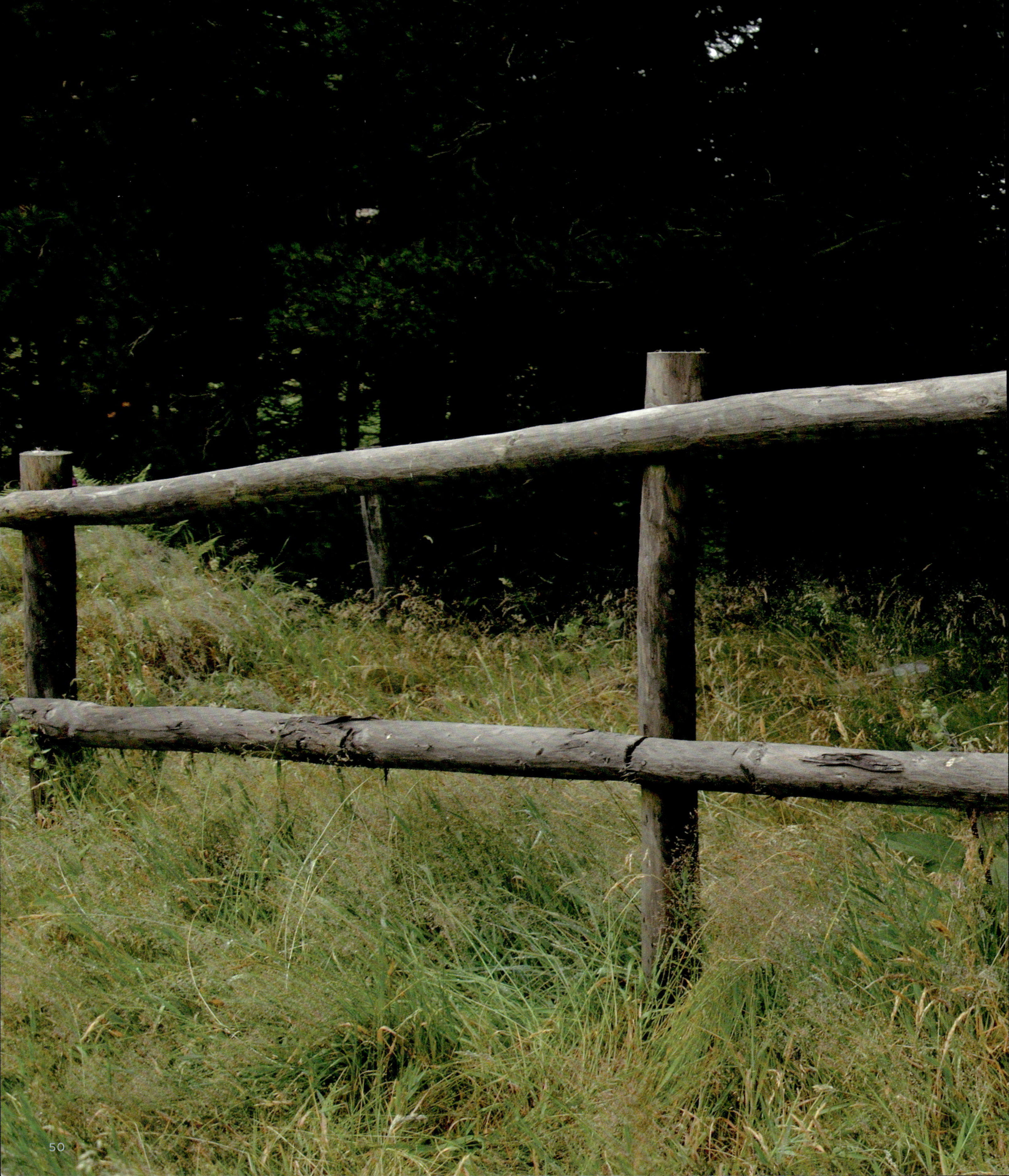

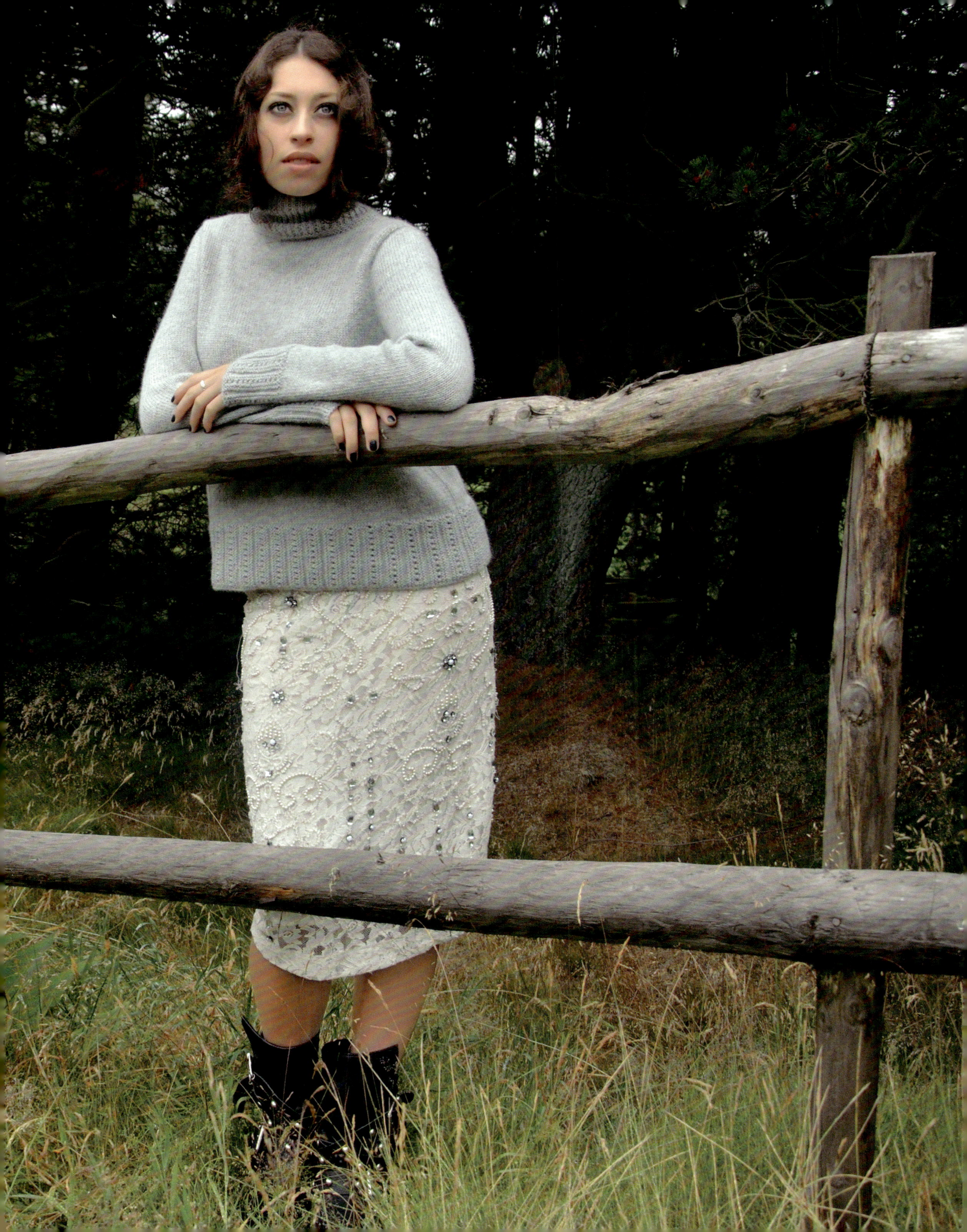

ALANA a cosy openwork scarf worn with pretty vintage and a faded parker coat

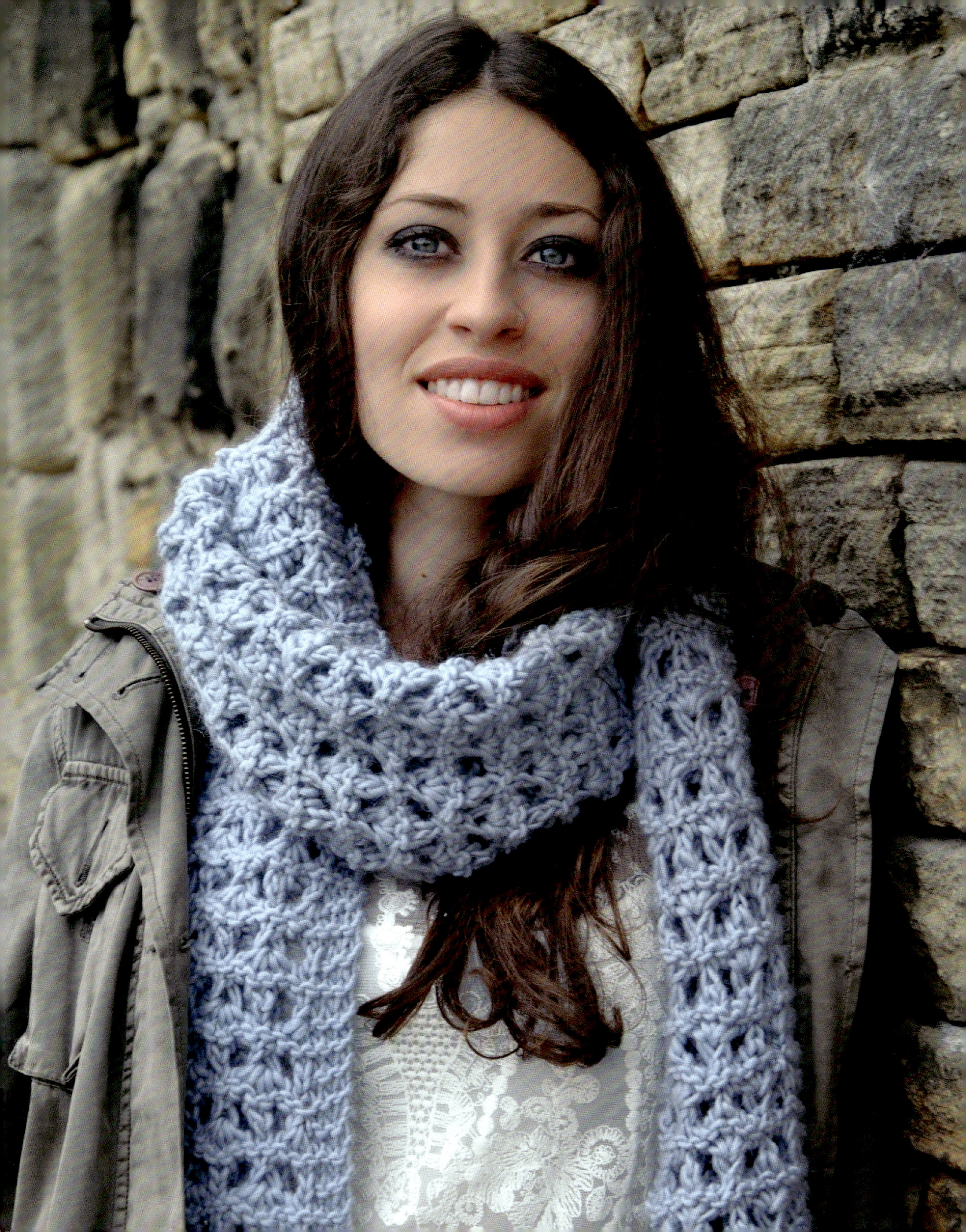

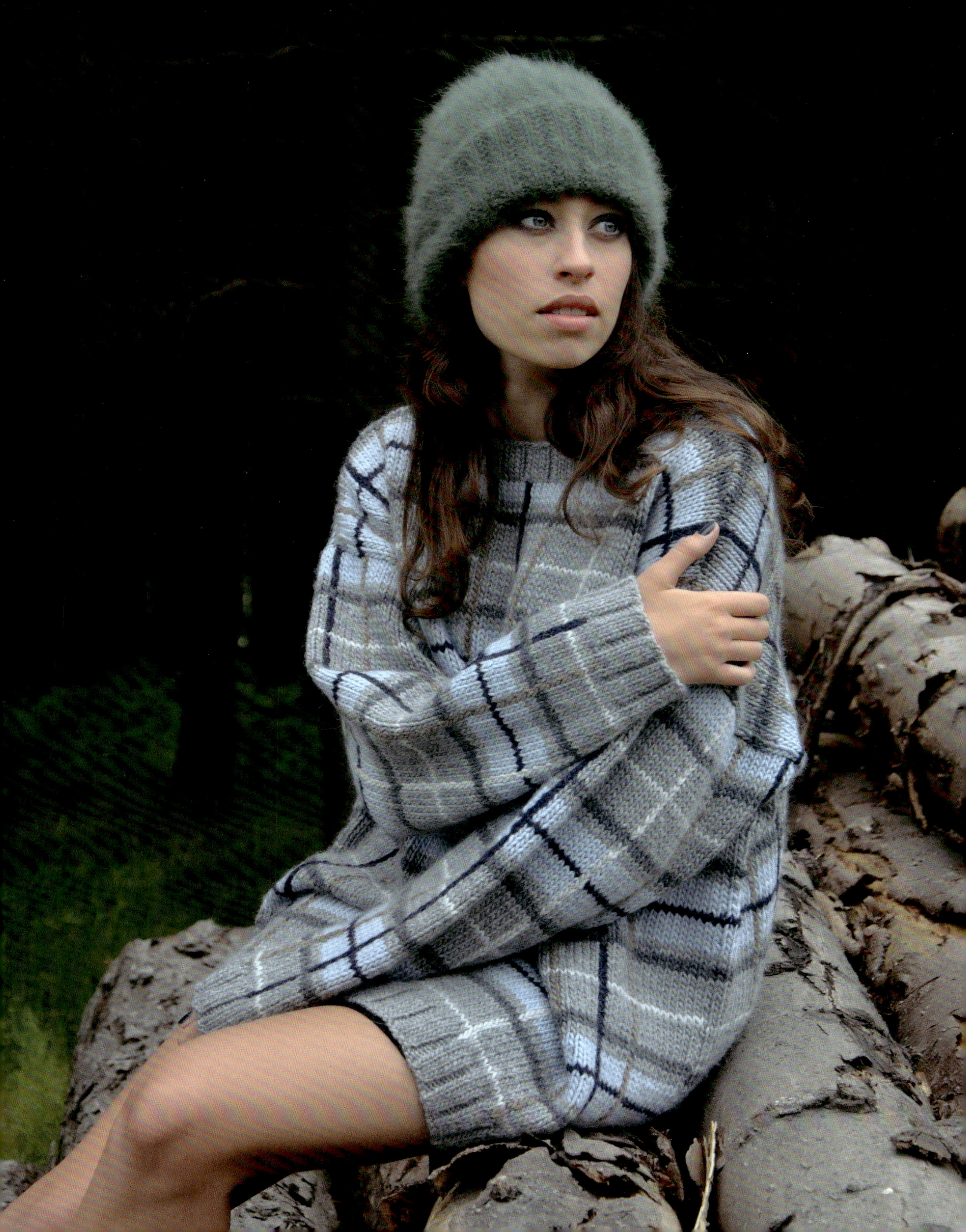

RIPLEY an oversized tartan sweater is given an edgy vibe, worn with **BRAM** ribbed hat

PATTERNS

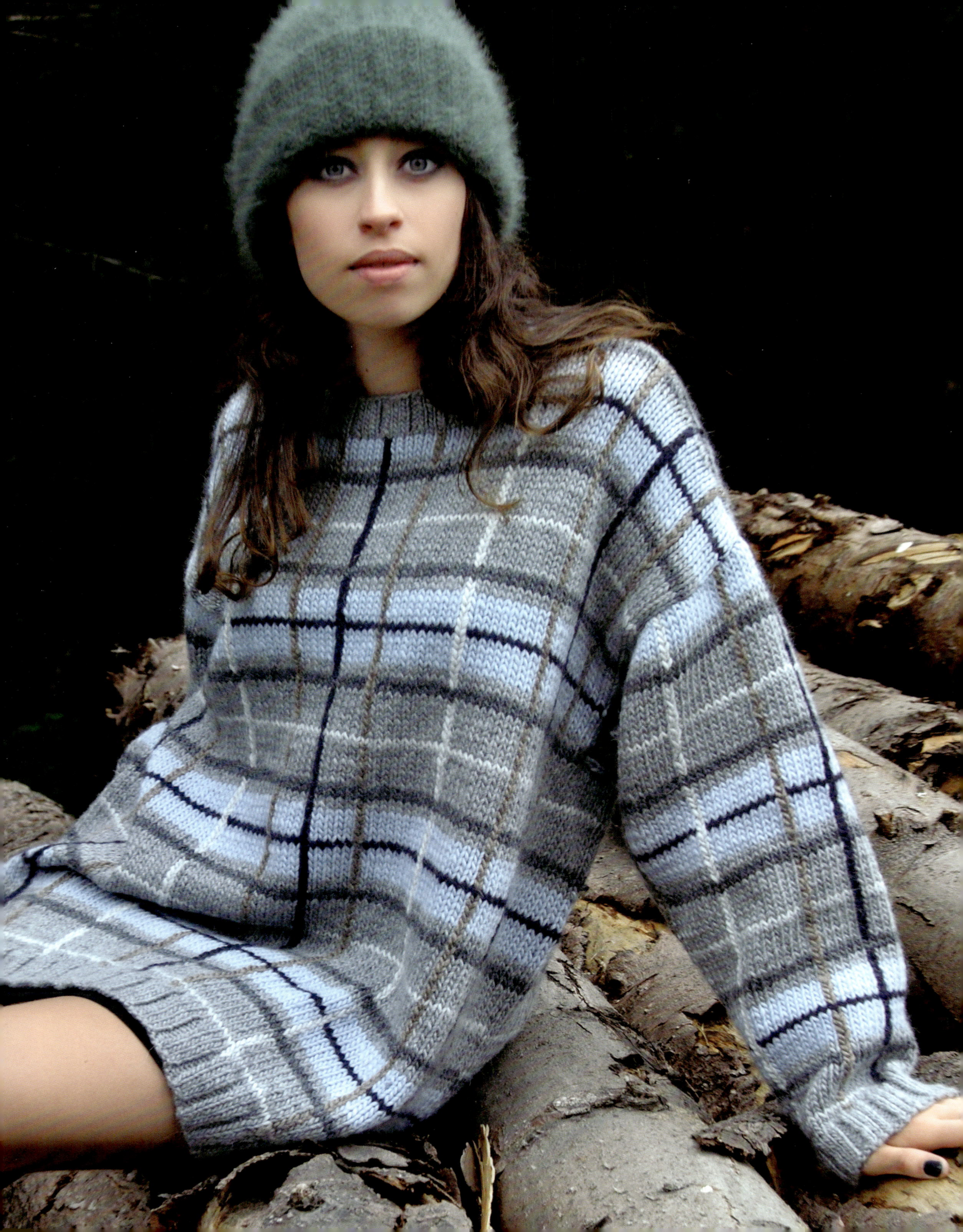

ECHO
Tweed duffle coat with cosy hood

Recommendation
Suitable for the knitter with a little experience
Please see pages 7 - 9 for photographs.

	XS	S	M	L	XL	XXL	
To fit bust	81	86	91	97	102	109	cm
	32	34	36	38	40	43	in

Rowan Tweed Aran
24 25 25 26 27 27 x50gm
Photographed in Malham

Needles
1 pair 4mm (no 8) (US 6) needles
1 pair 4½mm (no 7) (US 7) needles

Buttons – 9 large and 3 small

Tension
18 sts and 26 rows to 10 cm measured over double moss stitch using 4½mm (US 7) needles.

BACK
Cast on 105 (109: 113: 119: 123: 129) sts using 4½mm (US 7) needles.
Row 1 (RS): K1 (1: 1: 0: 0: 1), *P1, K1, rep from * to last 0 (0: 0: 1: 1: 0) st, P0 (0: 0: 1: 1: 0).
Row 2: As row 1.
Row 3: P1 (1: 1: 0: 0: 1), *K1, P1, rep from * to last 0 (0: 0: 1: 1: 0) st, K0 (0: 0: 1: 1: 0).
Row 4: As row 3.
These 4 rows form double moss st.
Cont in double moss st for a further 16 (16: 18: 18: 18: 18) rows, ending with a WS row.
Keeping patt correct, dec 1 st at each end of next and 6 foll 20th rows.
91 (95: 99: 105: 109: 115) sts.
Cont straight until back measures 63 (63: 64: 64: 64: 64) cm, ending with a **RS** row.
Shape armholes
Keeping patt correct, cast off 4 (4: 5: 5: 6: 6) sts at beg of next 2 rows.
83 (87: 89: 95: 97: 103) sts.
Dec 1 st at each end of next 1 (1: 1: 3: 3: 3) rows, then on foll 2 (3: 3: 3: 3: 5) alt rows, then on 2 foll 4th rows. 73 (75: 77: 79: 81: 83) sts.
Cont straight until armhole measures 19 (20: 20: 21: 22: 23) cm, ending with a WS row.
Shape shoulders
Row 1 (RS): Patt to last 8 (8: 8: 8: 9: 9) sts, wrap next st (by slipping next st from left needle onto right needle, taking yarn to opposite side of work between needles and then slipping same st back onto left needle - when working back across wrapped sts work the wrapped st and the wrapping loop tog as one st) and turn.
Row 2: Patt to last 8 (8: 8: 8: 9: 9) sts, wrap next st and turn.
Row 3: Patt to last 16 (16: 16: 16: 18: 18) sts, wrap next st and turn.
Row 4: Patt to last 16 (16: 16: 16: 18: 18) sts, wrap next st and turn.
Row 5: Patt to last 24 (24: 25: 25: 26: 27) sts, wrap next st and turn.
Row 6: Patt to last 24 (24: 25: 25: 26: 27) sts, wrap next st and turn.
Row 7: Knit to end.
Cast off all sts, placing markers 24 (24: 25: 25: 26: 27) sts in from both ends of row (to denote back neck).

POCKET LININGS (make 2)
Cast on 27 (27: 27: 29: 29: 29) sts using 4½mm (US 7) needles.
Row 1 (RS): P1, *K1, P1, rep from * to end.
Row 2: As row 1.
Row 3: K1, *P1, K1, rep from * to end.
Row 4: As row 3.
These 4 rows form double moss st.
Work in double moss st for a further 49 (49: 49: 51: 51: 51) rows, ending with a RS row.
Break yarn and leave sts on a holder.

LEFT FRONT
Cast on 57 (59: 61: 64: 66: 69) sts using 4½mm (US 7) needles.
Row 1 (RS): K1 (1: 1: 0: 0: 1), *P1, K1, rep from * to end.
Row 2: (K1, P1) 6 times, K3, *P1, K1, rep from * to last 0 (0: 0: 1: 1: 0) st, P0 (0: 0: 1: 1: 0).
Row 3: P1 (1: 1: 0: 0: 1), *K1, P1, rep from * to last 14 sts, (P1, K1) 7 times.
Row 4: (K1, P1) 6 times, K2, P1, *K1, P1, rep from * to last 0 (0: 0: 1: 1: 0) st, K0 (0: 0: 1: 1: 0).
These 4 rows set the sts – front opening edge 13 sts in moss st, side seam edge sts in double moss st, and one st in rev st st between.
Cont as set for a further 16 (16: 18: 18: 18: 18) rows, ending with a WS row.
Keeping patt correct, dec 1 st at beg of next and 3 foll 20th rows.
53 (55: 57: 60: 62: 65) sts.
Work 15 rows, ending with a WS row.
Place pocket
Next row (RS): Patt 7 (9: 11: 10: 12: 13) sts, cast off next 27 (27: 27: 29: 29: 29) sts in patt, patt to end.
Next row: Patt 19 (19: 19: 21: 21: 23) sts, with WS facing patt across 27 (27: 27: 29: 29: 29) sts of first pocket lining, patt to end.
Dec 1 st at beg of 3rd and 2 foll 20th rows. 50 (52: 54: 57: 59: 62) sts.
Cont straight until left front matches back to start of armhole shaping, ending with a **RS** row.
Shape armhole
Keeping patt correct, cast off 4 (4: 5: 5: 6: 6) sts at beg of next row. 46 (48: 49: 52: 53: 56) sts.
Work 1 row.

Dec 1 st at armhole edge of next 1 (1: 1: 3: 3: 3) rows, then on foll 2 (3: 3: 3: 3: 5) alt rows, then on 2 foll 4th rows.
41 (42: 43: 44: 45: 46) sts.
Cont straight until 9 (9: 9: 11: 11: 11) rows less have been worked than on back to start of shoulder shaping, ending with a **RS** row.
Shape front neck
Keeping patt correct, cast off 13 (14: 14: 14: 14: 14) sts at beg of next row.
28 (28: 29: 30: 31: 32) sts.
Dec 1 st at neck edge of next and foll 3 (3: 3: 4: 4: 4) alt rows. 24 (24: 25: 25: 26: 27) sts.
Work 1 row, ending with a WS row.
Shape shoulder
Row 1 (RS): Patt to end.
Row 2: Patt to last 8 (8: 8: 8: 9: 9) sts, wrap next st and turn.
Row 3: Patt to end.
Row 4: Patt to last 16 (16: 16: 16: 18: 18) sts, wrap next st and turn.
Row 5: Patt to end.
Cast off all 24 (24: 25: 25: 26: 27) sts.
Mark positions for 5 buttons along left front opening edge – first to come level with row 41 (41: 41: 43: 43: 43), last to come 3 cm below start of front neck shaping, and rem 3 buttons evenly spaced between.

RIGHT FRONT
Cast on 57 (59: 61: 64: 66: 69) sts using 4½mm (US 7) needles.
Row 1 (RS): K1, *P1, K1, rep from * to last 0 (0: 0: 1: 1: 0) st, P0 (0: 0: 1: 1: 0).
Row 2: K1 (1: 1: 0: 0: 1), *P1, K1, rep from * to last 14 sts, K2, (P1, K1) 6 times.
Row 3: (K1, P1) 7 times, P1, *K1, P1, rep from * to last 0 (0: 0: 1: 1: 0) st, K0 (0: 0: 1: 1: 0).
Row 4: P1 (1: 1: 0: 0: 1), *K1, P1, rep from * to last 14 sts, K2, (P1, K1) 6 times.
These 4 rows set the sts – front opening edge 13 sts in moss st, side seam edge sts in double moss st, and one st in rev st st between.
Cont as set for a further 16 (16: 18: 18: 18: 18) rows, ending with a WS row.
Keeping patt correct, dec 1 st at end of next row. 56 (58: 60: 63: 65: 68) sts.
Work 19 rows, ending with a WS row.
Next row (buttonhole row) (RS): Patt 5 sts, cast off 3 sts (to make a buttonhole – cast on 3 sts over these cast-off sts on next row), patt to last 2 sts, work 2 tog.
55 (57: 59: 62: 64: 67) sts.
Working a further 4 buttonholes in this way to correspond with positions marked for buttons on left front and noting that no further reference will be made to buttonholes, cont as folls:

Keeping patt correct, dec 1 st at end of 20th and foll 20th row. 53 (55: 57: 60: 62: 65) sts.
Work 15 rows, ending with a WS row.
Place pocket
Next row (RS): Patt 19 (19: 19: 21: 21: 23) sts, cast off next 27 (27: 27: 29: 29: 29) sts in patt, patt to end.
Next row: Patt 7 (9: 11: 10: 12: 13) sts, with WS facing patt across 27 (27: 27: 29: 29: 29) sts of second pocket lining, patt to end.
Complete to match left front, reversing shapings.

SLEEVES (both alike)
Cast on 45 (47: 49: 51: 53: 55) sts using 4mm (US 6) needles.
Row 1 (RS): P1, *K1, P1, rep from * to end.
Row 2: As row 1.
These 2 rows form moss st.
Work in moss st for a further 20 rows, ending with a WS row.
Change to 4½mm (US 7) needles.
Now work in double moss st as folls:
Row 1 (RS): P1, *K1, P1, rep from * to end.
Row 2: As row 1.
Row 3: Inc in first st, P1, *K1, P1, rep from * to last st, inc in last st. 47 (49: 51: 53: 55: 57) sts.
Row 4: P1, *K1, P1, rep from * to end.
These 4 rows form double moss st and beg sleeve shaping.
Cont in double moss st, shaping sides by inc 1 st at each end of 11th (11th: 13th: 13th: 11th: 11th) and every foll 12th (12th: 14th: 14th: 12th: 12th) row to 53 (53: 63: 63: 65: 65) sts, then on every foll 14th (14th: -: 16th: 14th: 14th) row until there are 59 (61: -: 65: 69: 71) sts, taking inc sts into patt.
Cont straight until sleeve measures 43 (44: 45: 46: 47: 48) cm, ending with a WS row.
Shape top
Keeping patt correct, cast off 4 (4: 5: 5: 6: 6) sts at beg of next 2 rows.
51 (53: 53: 55: 57: 59) sts.
Dec 1 st at each end of next 3 rows, then on foll alt row, then on 4 foll 4th rows.
35 (37: **37**: 39: 41: 43) sts.
Work 1 row.
Dec 1 st at each end of next and every foll alt row until 29 sts rem, then on foll 5 rows, ending with a WS row.
Cast off rem 19 sts.

MAKING UP
Press all pieces with a warm iron over a damp cloth.
On RS of work, join both shoulder seams using back stitch, to form seam on RS.

Hood
Cast on 25 sts using 4mm (US 6) needles.
Row 1 (RS): P1, *K1, P1, rep from * to end.
Row 2: Cast on 3 sts, work across these 3 sts and rem sts as folls: *K1, P1, rep from * to end. 28 sts.
These 2 rows set position of moss st.
Keeping moss st correct, cont as folls:
Cast on 3 sts at beg of 2nd and foll alt row, then 3 (3: 3: 4: 4: 4) sts at beg of 2 foll alt rows.
40 (40: 40: 42: 42: 42) sts.
Next row (buttonhole row) (RS): Patt 4 sts, *cast off next 2 sts (to make a buttonhole – cast on 2 sts over these cast-off sts on next row), patt until there are 9 sts on right needle after cast off, rep from * once more, cast off next 2 sts (to make 3rd buttonhole – cast on 2 sts over these cast-off sts on next row), patt to end.
Cast on 9 (11: 11: 12: 12: 12) sts at beg of next row, ending with a WS row.
49 (51: 51: 54: 54: 54) sts.
Now shape back seam of hood as folls:
Inc 1 st at end of next row and at same edge on foll 4 rows, then on foll alt row.
55 (57: 57: 60: 60: 60) sts.
Work 1 row, ending with a WS row.
Shape front opening edge
Cast off 16 (17: 17: 17: 17: 17) sts at beg and inc 1 st at end of next row.
40 (41: 41: 44: 44: 44) sts.
Dec 1 st at front opening edge of next 4 rows, then on foll 3 alt rows **and at same time** inc 1 st at back seam edge of 2nd and foll 2 alt rows, then on foll 4th row.
37 (38: 38: 41: 41: 41) sts.
Inc 1 st at back seam edge of 4th and foll 4th row, then on 3 foll 6th rows.
42 (43: 43: 46: 46: 46) sts.
Work 31 (31: 33: 33: 35: 35) rows, ending with a WS row.
Dec 1 st at back seam edge of next and 2 foll 4th rows, then on foll 3 alt rows, then on foll 3 rows, ending with a WS row.
33 (34: 34: 37: 37: 37) sts.
Now shape top of hood as folls:
Row 1 (RS): Patt to last 4 sts, wrap next st and turn.
Row 2: Patt to end.
Row 3: Patt to last 8 sts, wrap next st and turn.
Row 4: Patt to end.
Rows 5 and 6: As rows 3 and 4.
Rows 7 and 8: As rows 1 and 2.
This completes top of hood shaping.
Now working across all sts, cont as folls:
Work 1 row.

Inc 1 st at back seam edge of next 4 rows, then on foll 3 alt rows, then on 2 foll 4th rows.
42 (43: 43: 46: 46: 46) sts.
Work 31 (31: 33: 33: 35: 35) rows, ending with a WS row.
Dec 1 st at back seam edge of next and 3 foll 6th rows, then on foll 4th row.
37 (38: 38: 41: 41: 41) sts.
Work 3 rows, ending with a WS row.
Inc 1 st at front opening edge of next and foll 3 alt rows, then on foll 3 rows, ending with a WS row, **and at same time** dec 1 st at back seam edge of next and foll 4th row, then on foll 2 alt rows. 40 (41: 41: 44: 44: 44) sts.
Cast on 16 (17: 17: 17: 17: 17) sts at beg and dec 1 st at end of next row.
55 (57: 57: 60: 60: 60) sts.
Dec 1 st at back seam edge of 2nd and foll alt row, then on foll 4 rows, ending with a **RS** row.
49 (51: 51: 54: 54: 54) sts.
Cast off 9 (11: 11: 12: 12: 12) sts at beg of next row, 3 (3: 3: 4: 4: 4) sts at beg of foll 2 alt rows, then 3 sts at beg of foll 3 alt rows, ending with a WS row.
Cast off rem 25 sts.
Join back seam of hood. Matching back seam of hood to centre back neck and using photograph as a guide, sew hood to neck edge – ends of hood should extend approx 10 sts beyond front opening edges.

Pocket flaps (make 2)
Cast on 29 (29: 29: 31: 31: 31) sts using 4mm (US 6) needles.
Row 1 (RS): P1, *K1, P1, rep from * to end.
Row 2: As row 1.
These 2 rows form moss st.
Work in moss st for a further 16 rows, ending with a WS row.
Dec 1 st at each end of next row.
27 (27: 27: 29: 29: 29) sts.
Work 1 row.
Next row (buttonhole row) (RS): Work 2 tog, patt 10 (10: 10: 11: 11: 11) sts, cast off next 3 sts (to make a buttonhole – cast on 3 sts over these cast-off sts on next row), patt to last 2 sts, work 2 tog.
Dec 1 st at each end of 2nd and foll 3 alt rows, ending with a **RS** row.
Cast off rem 17 (17: 17: 19: 19: 19) sts in moss st (on **WS**).
Sew pocket linings in place on inside.
Using photograph as a guide, sew cast-on edge of pocket flap to front just above pocket opening edge and fold flap down over pocket opening. Attach a large button to front of pocket to correspond with buttonhole in flap to fasten pocket.

Sleeve tabs (make 2)
Cast on 11 sts using 4mm (US 6) needles.
Work in moss st as given for pocket flaps for 23 (24: 25: 26: 27: 28) cm, ending with a WS row.
Cast off in moss st.
Join side seams. Join sleeve seams, enclosing cast-on edge of sleeve tab in seam and positioning sleeve tab 5 cm up from sleeve cast-on edge. Insert sleeves into armholes. Sew on buttons, attaching 5 large buttons to left front to correspond with buttonholes in right front. Attach small buttons to left front neck section of hood to correspond with buttonholes in right front neck section. Wrap sleeve tab around sleeve as in photograph and attach a large button to each tab through both tab and sleeve to secure tab in place.

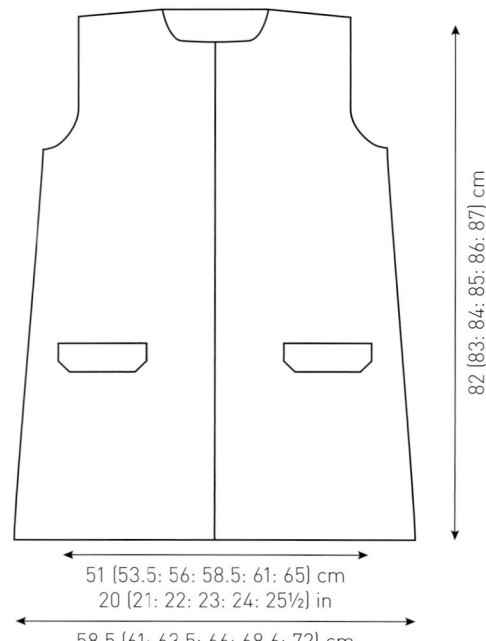

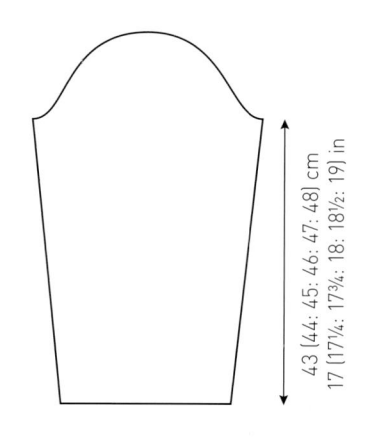

SHALE
Classic blazer with back vent

Recommendation
Suitable for the knitter with a little experience
Please see pages 10 & 11 for photographs.

	XS	S	M	L	XL	XXL	
To fit bust	81	86	91	97	102	109	cm
	32	34	36	38	40	43	in

Rowan Big Wool
9 9 10 10 11 12 x 100gm
Photographed in Glum

Needles
1 pair 8mm (no 0) (US 11) needles

Buttons – 2 large and 4 small

Tension
12 sts and 15 rows to 10 cm measured over double moss stitch using 8mm (US 11) needles.

BACK
Lower left back
Cast on 29 (30: 32: 33: 35: 37) sts using 8mm (US 11) needles.
Row 1 (RS): *P1, K1, rep from * to last 1 (0: 0: 1: 1: 1) st, P1 (0: 0: 1: 1: 1).
Row 2: P1 (0: 0: 1: 1: 1), *K1, P1, rep from * to end.
Row 3: *K1, P1, rep from * to last 1 (0: 0: 1: 1: 1) st, K1 (0: 0: 1: 1: 1).
Row 4: K1 (0: 0: 1: 1: 1), *P1, K1, rep from * to end.
These 4 rows form double moss st.
Cont in double moss st, dec 1 st at end of 11th and foll 8th row. 27 (28: 30: 31: 33: 35) sts.
Work 1 row, ending with a WS row.
Break yarn and leave sts on a holder.

Lower right back
Cast on 33 (34: 36: 37: 39: 41) sts using 8mm (US 11) needles.
Row 1 (RS): P1 (0: 0: 1: 1: 1), *K1, P1, rep from * to end.
Row 2: *P1, K1, rep from * to last 1 (0: 0: 1: 1: 1) st, P1 (0: 0: 1: 1: 1).
Row 3: K1 (0: 0: 1: 1: 1), *P1, K1, rep from * to end.
Row 4: *K1, P1, rep from * to last 1 (0: 0: 1: 1: 1) st, K1 (0: 0: 1: 1: 1).
These 4 rows form double moss st.
Cont in double moss st, dec 1 st at beg of 11th and foll 8th row. 31 (32: 34: 35: 37: 39) sts.
Work 1 row, ending with a WS row.

Join sections
Next row (RS): Patt to last 5 sts of lower left back, now holding RS of lower right back against WS of lower right back P tog first st of lower left back with next st of lower right back, (K tog next st of lower left back with next st of lower right back, P tog next st of lower left back with next st of lower right back) twice, patt rem 22 (23: 25: 26: 28: 30) sts of lower left back. 53 (55: 59: 61: 65: 69) sts.
Now working in double moss st across all sts, cont as folls:
Dec 1 st at each end of 6th row.
51 (53: 57: 59: 63: 67) sts.
Work 11 rows, ending with a WS row.
Inc 1 st at each end of next and 2 foll 8th rows.
57 (59: 63: 65: 69: 73) sts.
Cont straight until back measures 44 (44: 45: 45: 45: 45) cm, ending with a **RS** row.

Shape armholes
Keeping patt correct, cast off 3 sts at beg of next 2 rows. 51 (53: 57: 59: 63: 67) sts.
Dec 1 st at each end of next 3 (3: 3: 5: 5: 5) rows, then on foll 2 (2: 3: 2: 3: 4) alt rows. 41 (43: 45: 45: 47: 49) sts.
Cont straight until armhole measures 18 (19: 19: 20: 21: 22) cm, ending with a WS row.

Shape shoulders and back neck
Cast off 4 (5: 5: 5: 5: 5) sts at beg of next 2 rows. 33 (33: 35: 35: 37: 39) sts.
Next row (RS): Cast off 4 (5: 5: 5: 5: 5) sts, patt until there are 8 (7: 8: 7: 8: 9) sts on right needle and turn, leaving rem sts on a holder.
Work each side of neck separately.
Cast off 3 sts at beg of next row.
Cast off rem 5 (4: 5: 4: 5: 6) sts.
With RS facing, rejoin yarn to rem sts, cast off centre 9 (9: 9: 11: 11: 11) sts, patt to end.
Complete to match first side, reversing shapings.

POCKET LININGS (make 2)
Cast on 15 sts using 8mm (US 11) needles.
Row 1 (RS): P1, *K1, P1, rep from * to end.
Row 2: As row 1.
Row 3: K1, *P1, K1, rep from * to end.
Row 4: As row 3.
These 4 rows form double moss st.
Work in double moss st for a further 17 rows, ending with a RS row.
Break yarn and leave sts on a holder.

LEFT FRONT
Cast on 33 (34: 36: 37: 39: 41) sts using 8mm (US 11) needles.
Row 1 (RS): P1 (0: 0: 1: 1: 1), *K1, P1, rep from * to end.
Row 2: *P1, K1, rep from * to last 1 (0: 0: 1: 1: 1) st, P1 (0: 0: 1: 1: 1).
Row 3: K1 (0: 0: 1: 1: 1), *P1, K1, rep from * to end.
Row 4: *K1, P1, rep from * to last 1 (0: 0: 1: 1: 1) st, K1 (0: 0: 1: 1: 1).
These 4 rows form double moss st.
Cont in double moss st, dec 1 st at beg of 11th and foll 8th row. 31 (32: 34: 35: 37: 39) sts.
Work 7 rows, ending with a WS row.

Place pocket
Next row (RS): Work 2 tog, patt 3 (4: 4: 5: 5: 7) sts, cast off next 15 sts in patt, patt to end.

Next row: Patt 11 (11: 13: 13: 15: 15) sts, with **WS** facing patt across 15 sts of first pocket lining, patt rem 4 (5: 5: 6: 6: 8) sts. 30 (31: 33: 34: 36: 38) sts.
Work 10 rows, ending with a WS row.
Inc 1 st at beg of next and 2 foll 8th rows. 33 (34: 36: 37: 39: 41) sts.
Cont straight until left front matches back to start of armhole shaping, ending with a **RS** row.
Shape armhole
Keeping patt correct, cast off 3 sts at beg of next row. 30 (31: 33: 34: 36: 38) sts.
Work 1 row.
Dec 1 st at armhole edge of next 3 (3: 3: 5: 5: 5) rows, then on foll 2 (2: 3: 2: 3: 4) alt rows. 25 (26: 27: 27: 28: 29) sts.
Cont straight until 6 (6: 6: 8: 8: 8) rows less have been worked than on back to start of shoulder shaping, ending with a WS row.
Shape collar notch
Next row (RS): Patt to last 6 sts, cast off rem 6 sts in patt.
Break yarn.
With WS facing, rejoin yarn to rem sts and cont as folls:
Cast on 7 sts at beg of next row. 26 (27: 28: 28: 29: 30) sts.
Work 4 (4: 4: 6: 6: 6) rows, ending with a WS row.
Shape shoulder
Cast off 4 (5: 5: 5: 5: 5) sts at beg of next and foll alt row, then 5 (4: 5: 4: 5: 6) sts at beg of foll alt row.
Work on these rem 13 (13: 13: 14: 14: 14) sts only for back collar extension as folls: Inc 1 st at end of next row. 14 (14: 14: 15: 15: 15) sts.
Work a further 8 (8: 8: 10: 10: 10) rows, ending with a WS row.
Cast off 5 sts at beg of next and foll alt row.
Work 1 row.
Cast off rem 4 (4: 4: 5: 5: 5) sts.

RIGHT FRONT
Cast on 33 (34: 36: 37: 39: 41) sts using 8mm (US 11) needles.
Row 1 (RS): *P1, K1, rep from * to last 1 (0: 0: 1: 1: 1) st, P1 (0: 0: 1: 1: 1).
Row 2: P1 (0: 0: 1: 1: 1), *K1, P1, rep from * to end.
Row 3: *K1, P1, rep from * to last 1 (0: 0: 1: 1: 1) st, K1 (0: 0: 1: 1: 1).
Row 4: K1 (0: 0: 1: 1: 1), *P1, K1, rep from * to end.
These 4 rows form double moss st.
Cont in double moss st, dec 1 st at end of 11th and foll 8th row. 31 (32: 34: 35: 37: 39) sts.
Work 3 rows, ending with a WS row.
Next row (buttonhole row) (RS): K1, P1, K2tog tbl, yfwd (to make first buttonhole), patt to end.
Work 3 rows, ending with a WS row.
Place pocket
Next row (RS): Patt 11 (11: 13: 13: 15: 15) sts, cast off next 15 sts in patt, patt to last 2 sts, work 2 tog.
Next row: Patt 4 (5: 5: 6: 6: 8) sts, with **WS** facing patt across 15 sts of second pocket lining, patt rem 11 (11: 13: 13: 15: 15) sts. 30 (31: 33: 34: 36: 38) sts.
Work 10 rows, ending with a WS row.
Next row (buttonhole row) (RS): K1, P1, K2tog tbl, yfwd (to make second buttonhole), patt to last st, inc in last st.
Inc 1 st at end of 8th and foll 8th row. 33 (34: 36: 37: 39: 41) sts.
Complete to match left front, reversing shapings and working collar notch as folls:
Shape collar notch
Next row (RS): Cast off first 6 sts, turn and cast on 7 sts, turn and patt to end. 26 (27: 28: 29: 30) sts.

LEFT SLEEVE
Front cuff section
Cast on 20 (20: 21: 21: 22: 22) sts using 8mm (US 11) needles.
Row 1 (RS): *K1, P1, rep from * to last 0 (0: 1: 1: 0: 0) st, K0 (0: 1: 1: 0: 0).
Row 2: K0 (0: 1: 1: 0: 0), *P1, K1, rep from * to end.
Row 3: *P1, K1, rep from * to last 0 (0: 1: 1: 0: 0) st, P0 (0: 1: 1: 0: 0).
Row 4: P0 (0: 1: 1: 0: 0), *K1, P1, rep from * to end.
These 4 rows form double moss st.
Cont in double moss st for a further 8 rows, inc 1 st at end of 7th of these rows and ending with a WS row. 21 (21: 22: 22: 23: 23) sts.
Break yarn and leave sts on a holder.
Back cuff section
Cast on 12 (12: 13: 13: 14: 14) sts using 8mm (US 11) needles.
Row 1 (RS): K0 (0: 1: 1: 0: 0), *P1, K1, rep from * to end.
Row 2: *K1, P1, rep from * to last 0 (0: 1: 1: 0: 0) st, K0 (0: 1: 1: 0: 0).
Row 3: P0 (0: 1: 1: 0: 0), *K1, P1, rep from * to end.
Row 4: *P1, K1, rep from * to last 0 (0: 1: 1: 0: 0) st, P0 (0: 1: 1: 0: 0).
These 4 rows form double moss st.
Cont in double moss st for a further 8 rows, inc 1 st at beg of 7th of these rows and ending with a WS row. 13 (13: 14: 14: 15: 15) sts.
Join sections
Next row (RS): Patt to last 3 sts of back cuff section, now holding RS of back cuff section against WS of front cuff section K tog first st of front cuff section with next st of back cuff section, P tog next st of front cuff section with next st of back cuff section K tog next st of front cuff section with last st of back cuff section, patt rem 18 (18: 19: 19: 20: 20) sts of front cuff section. 31 (31: 33: 33: 35: 35) sts.
**Now working in double moss st across all sts, cont as folls:
Inc 1 st at each end of 12th (8th: 12th: 10th: 10th: 8th) and 2 (1: 2: 3: 3: 4) foll 14th (10th: 16th: 12th: 12th: 10th) rows, then on 0 (2: 0: 0: 0: 0) foll 12th rows, taking inc sts into patt. 37 (39: 39: 41: 43: 45) sts.
Cont straight until sleeve measures 43 (44: 45: 46: 47: 48) cm, ending with a WS row.
Shape top
Keeping patt correct, cast off 3 sts at beg of next 2 rows. 31 (33: 33: 35: 37: 39) sts.
Dec 1 st at each end of next and foll 3 alt rows, then on foll 4th row. 21 (23: 23: 25: 27: 29) sts.
Work 1 row.
Dec 1 st at each end of next and every foll alt row until 17 sts rem, then on foll 3 rows, ending with a WS row.
Cast off rem 11 sts.

RIGHT SLEEVE
Back cuff section
Cast on 12 (12: 13: 13: 14: 14) sts using 8mm (US 11) needles.
Work in double moss st at given for front cuff section of left sleeve for 12 rows, inc 1 st at end of 11th of these rows and ending with a WS row. 13 (13: 14: 14: 15: 15) sts.
Break yarn and leave sts on a holder.
Front cuff section
Cast on 20 (20: 21: 21: 22: 22) sts using 8mm (US 11) needles.
Work in double moss st as given for back cuff section of left sleeve for 12 rows, inc 1 st at beg of 11th of these rows and ending with a WS row. 21 (21: 22: 22: 23: 23) sts.
Join sections
Next row (RS): Patt to last 3 sts of front cuff section, now holding WS of front cuff section against RS of back cuff section K tog next st of front cuff section with first st of back cuff section, P tog next st of front cuff section with next st of back cuff section K tog last st of front cuff section with next st of back cuff section, patt rem 10 (10: 11: 11: 12: 12) sts of back cuff section. 31 (31: 33: 33: 35: 35) sts.
Complete as given for left sleeve from **.

Continued on next page...

SMOKY
Slouchy striped hat

Recommendation
Suitable for the knitter with a little experience
Please see pages 12, 15 & 38 for photographs.

Rowan Baby Alpaca DK
A Jacob   2   x 50gm
B Lincoln   1   x 50gm

Needles
1 pair 3mm (no 11) (US 2/3) needles
1 pair 3¾mm (no 9) (US 5) needles

Tension
23 sts and 31 rows to 10 cm measured over stocking stitch using 3¾mm (US 5) needles.

HAT
Cast on 131 sts using 3mm (US 2/3) needles and yarn A.
Row 1 (RS): K2, *P2, K3, rep from * to last 4 sts, P2, K2.
Row 2: P2, *K2, P3, rep from * to last 4 sts, K2, P2.
These 2 rows form rib.
Work in rib for a further 18 rows, dec 1 st at each end of last row and ending with a WS row.
129 sts.
Change to 3¾mm (US 5) needles.
Beg with a K row, now work in st st as folls:
Work 2 rows.
Join in yarn B.
Now work in stripes as folls:
Using yarn B, work 2 rows.
Using yarn A, work 6 rows.
Last 8 rows form striped st st.
Cont in striped st st for a further 42 rows, ending after 2 rows using yarn B and with a WS row.
Break off yarn B and complete hat using yarn A **only**.
Work 2 rows, ending with a WS row.
Shape top
Row 1 (RS): K1, *K2tog, rep from * to end. 65 sts.
Row 2: Purl.
Row 3: K1, *K2tog, rep from * to end. 33 sts.
Row 4: Purl.
Row 5: K1, *K2tog, rep from * to end.
Break yarn and thread through rem 17 sts.
Pull up tight and fasten off securely.
Sew back seam.

SHALE – Continued from previous page.

MAKING UP
Press all pieces with a warm iron over a damp cloth.
Join both shoulder seams using back stitch or mattress stitch if preferred. Join shaped cast-off ends of back collar extensions, then sew one edge to back neck edge.
Sew pocket linings in place on inside.
Join side seams. Join sleeve seams.
Insert sleeves into armholes.
Sew on buttons, attaching large buttons to left front to correspond with buttonholes in right front. Overlap ends of cuff sections for 3 sts and, using photograph as a guide, attach 2 small buttons to each cuff through both layers to secure cuff opening.

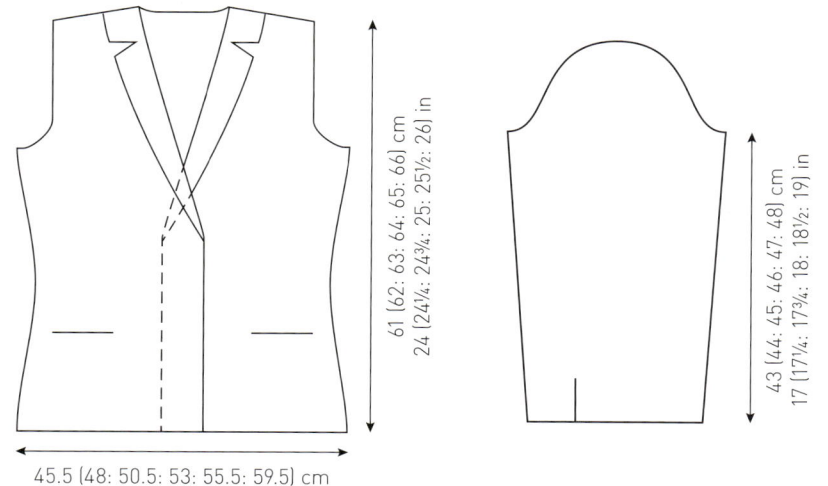

45.5 (48: 50.5: 53: 55.5: 59.5) cm
18 (19: 20: 21: 22: 23¼)

61 (62: 63: 64: 65: 66) cm
24 (24¼: 24¾: 25: 25½: 26) in

43 (44: 45: 46: 47: 48) cm
17 (17¼: 17¾: 18: 18½: 19) in

TEMPEST
Dolman sleeved tunic

Recommendation
Suitable for the knitter with a little experience
Please see pages 12 - 15 for photographs.

	XS	S	M	L	XL	XXL	
To fit bust	81	86	91	97	102	109	cm
	32	34	36	38	40	43	in

Rowan Alpaca Cotton
7 8 8 9 9 10x 50gm
Photographed in Storm

Needles
1 pair 4½mm (no 7) (US 7) needles
1 pair 5½mm (no 5) (US 9) needles

Tension
16 sts and 22 rows to 10 cm measured over stocking stitch using 5½mm (US 9) needles.

BACK
Cast on 96 (101: 106: 111: 116: 123) sts using 4½mm (US 7) needles.
Row 1 (RS): K2 (2: 2: 2: 2: 3), P2, *K3, P2, rep from * to last 2 (2: 2: 2: 2: 3) sts, K2 (2: 2: 2: 2: 3).
Row 2: P2 (2: 2: 2: 2: 3), K2, *P3, K2, rep from * to last 2 (2: 2: 2: 2: 3) sts, P2 (2: 2: 2: 2: 3).
These 2 rows form rib.
Cont in rib for a further 19 rows, ending with a **RS** row.
Change to 5½mm (US 9) needles.
Row 22 (WS): P2 (2: 2: 2: 2: 3), K2tog, *P3, K2tog, rep from * to last 2 (2: 2: 2: 2: 3) sts, P2 (2: 2: 2: 2: 3). 77 (81: 85: 89: 93: 99) sts.
Beg with a K row, now work in st st throughout as folls:
Cont straight until back measures 26 (26.5: 27: 27.5: 28: 28.5) cm, ending with a WS row.
Inc 1 st at each end of next and foll 10th row, then on 2 foll 8th rows, then on foll 6th row, then on 3 foll 4th rows, then on foll 5 alt rows, then on foll 7 rows, ending with a WS row.
117 (121: 125: 129: 133: 139) sts.
Cast on 2 sts at beg of next 2 rows, then 3 sts at beg of foll 6 rows, then 2 sts at beg of next 2 rows.
143 (147: 151: 155: 159: 165) sts.
Place markers at both ends of last row (to denote base of armhole opening).**
Cont straight until work measures 15.5 (16: 16.5: 17: 17.5: 18) cm from markers, ending with a WS row.
Shape shoulders
Cast off 6 (6: 6: 7: 7: 7) sts at beg of next 8 (6: 2: 12: 12: 6) rows, then 7 (7: 7: -: -: 8) sts at beg of foll 4 (6: 10: -: -: 6) rows.
67 (69: 69: 71: 75: 75) sts.
Shape back neck
Next row (RS): Cast off 7 (7: 7: 7: 8: 8) sts, K until there are 11 (11: 11: 11: 12: 12) sts on right needle and turn, leaving rem sts on a holder.
Work each side of neck separately.
Cast off 4 sts at beg of next row.
Cast off rem 7 (7: 7: 7: 8: 8) sts.
With RS facing, rejoin yarn to rem sts, cast off centre 31 (33: 33: 35: 35: 35) sts, K to end.
Complete to match first side, reversing shapings.

FRONT
Work as given for back to **.
Cont straight until 0 (0: 0: 2: 2: 2) rows less have been worked than on back to start of shoulder shaping, ending with a WS row.
Shape shoulders and front neck
Next row (RS): Cast off 6 (6: 6: 0: 0: 0) sts, K until there are 54 (55: 57: 65: 67: 70) sts on right needle and turn, leaving rem sts on a holder.
Work each side of neck separately.
Dec 1 st at neck edge of next 6 rows, then on foll 2 (2: 2: 3: 3: 3) alt rows **and at same time** cast off 6 (6: 7: 7: 7: 7) sts at beg of 2nd and foll 2 (1: 4: 5: 5: 2) alt rows, then 7 (7: -: -: -: 8) sts at beg of foll 2 (3: -: -: -: 3) alt rows.
14 (14: 14: 14: 16: 16) sts.
Work 1 row.
Cast off 7 (7: 7: 7: 8: 8) sts at beg of next row.
Work 1 row.
Cast off rem 7 (7: 7: 7: 8: 8) sts.
With RS facing, rejoin yarn to rem sts, cast off centre 23 (25: 25: 25: 25: 25) sts, K to end. 60 (61: 63: 65: 67: 70) sts.
Complete to match first side, reversing shapings.

MAKING UP
Press all pieces with a warm iron over a damp cloth.
Join right shoulder/overarm seam using back stitch or mattress stitch if preferred.
Neckband
With RS facing and using 4½mm (US 7) needles, pick up and knit 14 (14: 14: 15: 15: 15) sts down left side of neck, 23 (25: 25: 25: 25: 25) sts from front, 14 (14: 14: 15: 15: 15) sts up right side of neck, then 42 (44: 44: 46: 46: 46) sts from back.
93 (97: 97: 101: 101: 101) sts.
Row 1 (WS): P2, inc knitwise on next st, *P3, inc knitwise in next st, rep from * to last 2 sts, P2.
116 (121: 121: 126: 126: 126) sts.
Row 2: K2, P2, *K3, P2, rep from * to last 2 sts, K2.
Row 3: P2, K2, *P3, K2, rep from * to last 2 sts, P2.
Row 4: As row 2.

Row 5: P2, K2tog, *P3, K2tog, rep from * to last 2 sts, P2.
93 (97: 97: 101: 101: 101) sts.
Now cast off in rib.
Join left shoulder/overarm and neckband seam.

Sleeves (both alike)
With RS facing and using 5½mm (US 9) needles, pick up and knit 51 (53: 55: 57: 59: 61) sts evenly along armhole opening edge between markers.
Beg with a P row, work in st st as folls:
Work 5 rows, ending with a WS row.
Next row (RS): K3, K2tog, K to last 5 sts, K2tog tbl, K3.
Working all decreases as set by last row, dec 1 st at each end of 4th and 2 (2: 2: 1: 0: 0) foll 4th rows, then on 2 (2: 1: 2: 3: 2) foll 6th rows, then on 0 (0: 1: 1: 1: 2) foll 8th rows.
39 (41: 43: 45: 47: 49) sts.
Work 2 (4: 4: 4: 4: 4) rows, ending with a **RS** row.
Next row (WS): P3 (4: 5: 2: 3: 4), inc knitwise in next st, *P3, inc knitwise in next st, rep from * to last 3 (4: 5: 2: 3: 4) sts, P3 (4: 5: 2: 3: 4).
48 (50: 52: 56: 58: 60) sts.
Change to 4½mm (US 7) needles.
Next row: K3 (4: 5: 2: 3: 4), P2, *K3, P2, rep from * to last 3 (4: 5: 2: 3: 4) sts, K3 (4: 5: 2: 3: 4).
Next row: P3 (4: 5: 2: 3: 4), K2, *P3, K2, rep from * to last 3 (4: 5: 2: 3: 4) sts, P3 (4: 5: 2: 3: 4).
Last 2 rows form rib.
Cont in rib, dec 1 st at each end of 3rd and foll 10th row.
44 (46: 48: 52: 54: 56) sts.
Cont straight until sleeve measures 28 (29: 30: 31: 32: 33) cm from pick-up row, ending with a **RS** row.
Next row (WS): P1 (2: 3: 0: 1: 2), K2tog, *P3, K2tog, rep from * to last 1 (2: 3: 0: 1: 2) sts, P1 (2: 3: 0: 1: 2).
35 (37: 39: 41: 43: 45) sts.
Cast off in rib.
Join side and sleeve seams.

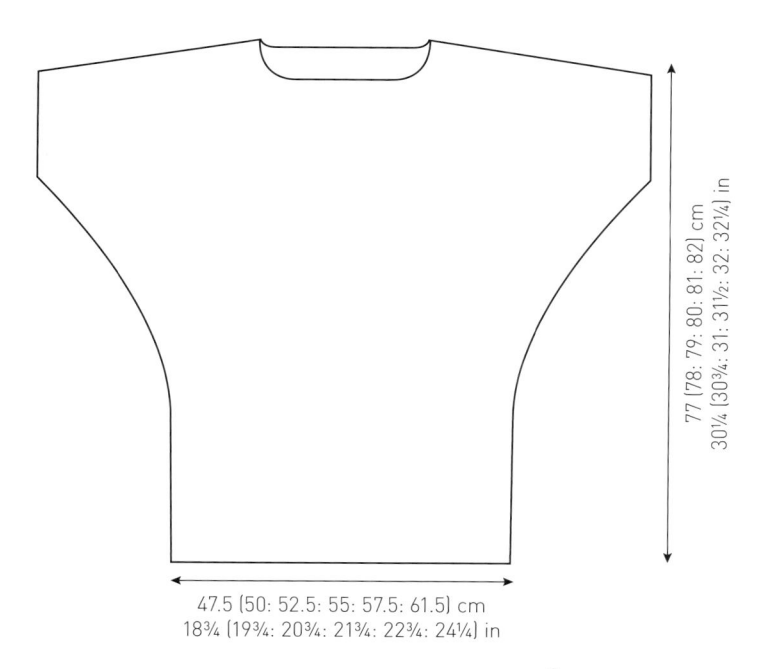

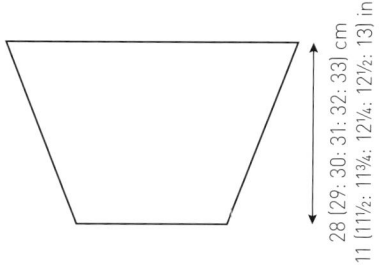

77 (78: 79: 80: 81: 82) cm
30¼ (30¾: 31: 31½: 32: 32¼) in

47.5 (50: 52.5: 55: 57.5: 61.5) cm
18¾ (19¾: 20¾: 21¾: 22¾: 24¼) in

28 (29: 30: 31: 32: 33) cm
11 (11½: 11¾: 12¼: 12½: 13) in

WEALD
A-line guernsey style sweater

Recommendation
Suitable for the knitter with a little experience
Please see pages 16 & 17 for photographs.

	XS	S	M	L	XL	XXL	
To fit bust	81	86	91	97	102	109	cm
	32	34	36	38	40	43	in

Rowan Pure Wool Aran
7 8 8 8 9 9 x 100gm
Photographed in Ivory

Needles
1 pair 4mm (no 8) (US 6) needles
1 pair 5mm (no 6) (US 8) needles
Cable needle

Tension
18 sts and 26 rows to 10 cm measured over stocking stitch using 5mm (US 8) needles.

Special abbreviations
C6B = slip next 3 sts onto cn and leave at back of work, K3, then K3 from cn; **C6F** = slip next 3 sts onto cn and leave at front of work, K3, then K3 from cn; **cn** = cable needle.

BACK
Cast on 120 (125: 130: 135: 140: 150) sts using 4mm (US 6) needles.
Row 1 (RS): K4, P2, *K3, P2, rep from * to last 4 sts, K4.
Row 2: K6, *P3, K2, rep from * to last 4 sts, K4.
These 2 rows set the sts – 4 sts in g st at each end of row with sts between in rib.
Cont as set for a further 21 rows, ending with a **RS** row.
Change to 5mm (US 8) needles.
Row 24 (WS): Patt 4 (4: 4: 9: 9: 4) sts, K2tog, *P3, K2tog, rep from * to last 4 (4: 4: 9: 9: 4) sts, patt 4 (4: 4: 9: 9: 4) sts.
97 (101: 105: 111: 115: 121) sts.
Beg with a K row, work in st st for 2 rows, ending with a WS row.
Now work border as folls:
Row 1 (RS): K2tog, K6 (0: 2: 5: 7: 2), P1, *K7, P1, rep from * to last 8 (2: 4: 7: 9: 4) sts, K6 (0: 2: 5: 7: 2), K2tog.
95 (99: 103: 109: 113: 119) sts.
Row 2: P0 (0: 2: 5: 0: 2), K0 (1: 1: 1: 0: 1), P0 (1: 1: 1: 1: 1), *K1, P5, K1, P1, rep from * to last 7 (1: 3: 6: 0: 3) sts, K1 (1: 1: 1: 0: 1), P5 (0: 2: 5: 0: 2), K1 (0: 0: 0: 0: 0).
Row 3: K1 (3: 1: 0: 2: 1), P1, *K3, P1, rep from * to last 1 (3: 1: 0: 2: 1) sts, K1 (3: 1: 0: 2: 1).
Row 4: K0 (0: 1: 0: 0: 1), P2 (4: 5: 1: 3: 5), *K1, P1, K1, P5, rep from * to last 5 (7: 1: 4: 6: 1) sts, K1, P1 (1: 0: 1: 1: 0), K1 (0: 0: 1: 1: 0), P2 (4: 0: 1: 3: 0).
Row 5: K3 (5: 7: 2: 4: 7), P1, *K7, P1, rep from * to last 3 (5: 7: 2: 4: 7) sts, K3 (5: 7: 2: 4: 7).
Row 6: As row 4.
Row 7: As row 3.
Row 8: As row 2.
Row 9: K7 (1: 3: 6: 0: 3), P1, *K7, P1, rep from * to last 7 (1: 3: 6: 0: 3) sts, K7 (1: 3: 6: 0: 3).
These 9 rows complete border.
Beg with a P row, cont in st st as folls:
Work 3 (3: 5: 5: 5: 5) rows, ending with a WS row.
Next row (RS): K3, K2tog, K to last 5 sts, K2tog tbl, K3.
Working all side seam decreases as set by last row, dec 1 st at each end of 12th and 4 foll 12th rows. 83 (87: 91: 97: 101: 107) sts.
Work 1 row, ending with a WS row.
Now work border for yoke as folls:
Row 1 (RS): K1 (3: 5: 0: 2: 5), P1, *K7, P1, rep from * to last 1 (3: 5: 0: 2: 5) sts, K1 (3: 5: 0: 2: 5).
Row 2: P0 (2: 4: 0: 1: 4), K1 (1: 1: 0: 1: 1), P1, *K1, P5, K1, P1, rep from * to last 1 (3: 5: 0: 2: 5) sts, K1 (1: 1: 0: 1: 1), P0 (2: 4: 0: 1: 4).
Row 3: K3 (1: 3: 2: 0: 3), P1, *K3, P1, rep from * to last 3 (1: 3: 2: 0: 3) sts, K3 (1: 3: 2: 0: 3).
Row 4: K0 (1: 0: 0: 0: 0), P4 (5: 0: 3: 5: 0), *K1, P1, K1, P5, rep from * to last 7 (1: 3: 6: 0: 3) sts, K1 (1: 1: 1: 0: 1), P1 (0: 1: 1: 0: 1), K1 (0: 1: 1: 1: 0: 1), P4 (0: 0: 3: 0: 0).
Row 5: K5 (7: 1: 4: 6: 1), P1, *K7, P1, rep from * to last 5 (7: 1: 4: 6: 1) sts, K5 (7: 1: 4: 6: 1).
Row 6: P1 (3: 5: 0: 2: 5), K1, *P7, K1, rep from * to last 1 (3: 5: 0: 2: 5) sts, P1 (3: 5: 0: 2: 5).
Row 7: K0 (2: 4: 0: 1: 4), P1 (1: 1: 0: 1: 1), K1, *P1, K5, P1, K1, rep from * to last 1 (3: 5: 0: 2: 5) sts, P1 (1: 1: 0: 1: 1), K0 (2: 4: 0: 1: 4).
Row 8: P3 (1: 3: 2: 0: 3), K1, *P3, K1, rep from * to last 3 (1: 3: 2: 0: 3) sts, P3 (1: 3: 2: 0: 3).
Row 9: P0 (1: 0: 0: 0: 0), K4 (5: 0: 3: 5: 0), *P1, K1, P1, K5, rep from * to last 7 (1: 3: 6: 0: 3) sts, P1 (1: 1: 1: 0: 1), K1 (0: 1: 1: 0: 1), P1 (0: 1: 1: 1: 0: 1), K4 (0: 0: 3: 0: 0).
Row 10: P5 (7: 1: 4: 6: 1), K1, *P7, K1, rep from * to last 5 (7: 1: 4: 6: 1) sts, P5 (7: 1: 4: 6: 1).
Row 11: Knit.
Rows 12 to 15: Purl.
Row 16: P21 (23: 25: 28: 30: 33), M1P, P2, M1P, P37, M1P, P2, M1P, P21 (23: 25: 28: 30: 33). 87 (91: 95: 101: 105: 111) sts.
These 16 rows complete border for yoke.
Beg and ending rows as indicated, working chart rows 1 and 2 **once only** and then repeating the 16 and 18 row patt repeats throughout, now work in patt from chart for yoke as folls:
Work 12 rows, ending with a WS row.
Shape armholes
Keeping patt correct, cast off 2 (3: 3: 4: 4: 5) sts at beg of next 2 rows.
83 (85: 89: 93: 97: 101) sts.
Dec 1 st at each end of next 3 (3: 3: 3: 5: 5) rows, then on foll 1 (1: 2: 3: 2: 3) alt rows, then on foll 4th row.
73 (75: 77: 79: 81: 83) sts.
Cont straight until armhole measures 18 (19: 19: 20: 21: 22) cm, ending with a WS row.

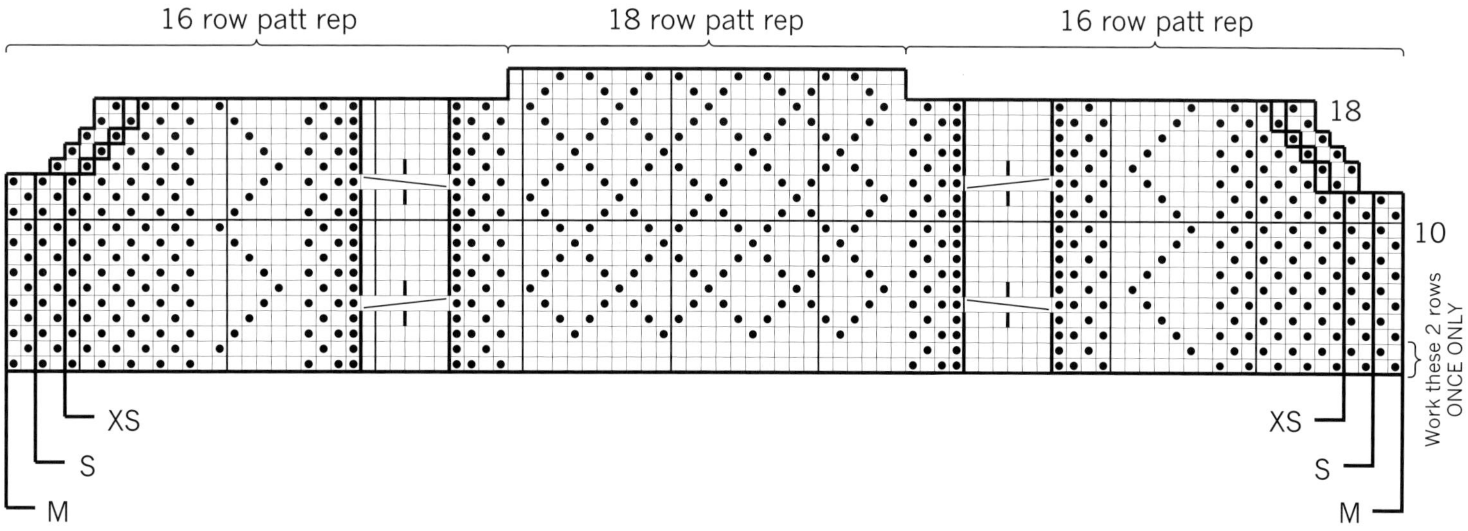

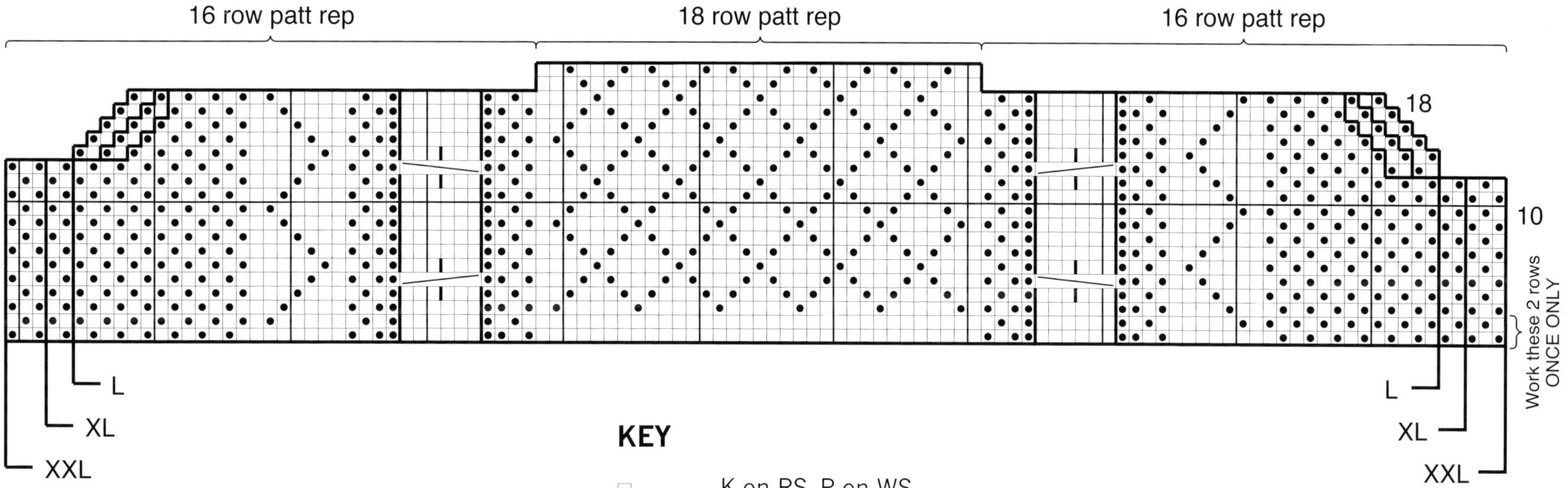

KEY

- □ K on RS, P on WS
- • P on RS, K on WS
- C6B
- C6F

Shape shoulders and back neck
Cast off 6 (6: 7: 7: 7: 7) sts at beg of next 2 rows. 61 (63: 63: 65: 67: 69) sts.
Next row (RS): Cast off 6 (6: 7: 7: 7: 7) sts, patt until there are 13 (13: 12: 12: 13: 14) sts on right needle and turn, leaving rem sts on a holder.
Work each side of neck separately.
Cast off 4 sts at beg of next row.
Cast off rem 9 (9: 8: 8: 9: 10) sts, dec 2 sts at top of cable.
With RS facing, rejoin yarn to rem sts, cast off centre 23 (25: 25: 27: 27: 27) sts, patt to end.
Complete to match first side, reversing shapings.

FRONT
Work as given for back until 12 (12: 12: 14: 14: 14) rows less have been worked than on back to start of shoulder shaping, ending with a WS row.
Shape front neck
Next row (RS): Patt 28 (28: 29: 30: 31: 32) sts and turn, leaving rem sts on a holder.
Work each side of neck separately.
Keeping patt correct, dec 1 st at neck edge of next 4 rows, then on foll 3 (3: 3: 4: 4: 4) alt rows. 21 (21: 22: 22: 23: 24) sts.
Work 1 row, ending with a WS row.
Shape shoulder
Cast off 6 (6: 7: 7: 7: 7) sts at beg of next and foll alt row.
Work 1 row.
Cast off rem 9 (9: 8: 8: 9: 10) sts, dec 2 sts at top of cable.
With RS facing, rejoin yarn to rem sts, cast off centre 17 (19: 19: 19: 19: 19) sts, patt to end.
Complete to match first side, reversing shapings.

SLEEVES (both alike)
Cast on 51 (53: 57: 59: 61: 63) sts using 4mm (US 6) needles.
Row 1 (RS): K2 (3: 0: 1: 2: 3), P2, *K3, P2, rep from * to last 2 (3: 0: 1: 2: 3) sts, K2 (3: 0: 1: 2: 3).
Row 2: P2 (3: 0: 1: 2: 3), K2, *P3, K2, rep from * to last 2 (3: 0: 1: 2: 3) sts, P2 (3: 0: 1: 2: 3).
These 2 rows form rib.
Work in rib for a further 19 rows, ending with a **RS** row.
Change to 5mm (US 8) needles.
Row 22 (WS): P2 (3: 0: 1: 2: 3), K2tog, *P3, K2tog, rep from * to last 2 (3: 0: 1: 2: 3) sts, P2 (3: 0: 1: 2: 3). 41 (43: 45: 47: 49: 51) sts.
Beg with a K row, work in st st for 2 rows, ending with a WS row.
Now work border as folls:
Row 1 (RS): Inc in first st, K3 (4: 5: 6: 7: 0), P1, *K7, P1, rep from * to last 4 (5: 6: 7: 8: 1) sts, K3 (4: 5: 6: 7: 0), inc in last st. 43 (45: 47: 49: 51: 53) sts.
Row 2: P4 (5: 0: 0: 0: 1), K1 (1: 0: 0: 1: 1), P1 (1: 0: 1: 1: 1), *K1, P5, K1, P1, rep from * to last 5 (6: 7: 0: 1: 2) sts, K1 (1: 1: 0: 1: 1), P4 (5: 5: 0: 0: 1), K0 (0: 1: 0: 0: 0).
Row 3: K3 (0: 1: 2: 3: 0), P1, *K3, P1, rep from * to last 3 (0: 1: 2: 3: 0) sts, K3 (0: 1: 2: 3: 0).
Row 4: P0 (1: 2: 3: 4: 5), *K1, P1, K1, P5, rep from * to last 3 (4: 5: 6: 7: 0) sts, K1 (1: 1: 1: 1: 0), P1 (1: 1: 1: 1: 0), K1 (1: 1: 1: 1: 0), P0 (1: 2: 3: 4: 5).
Row 5: K1 (2: 3: 4: 5: 6), P1, *K7, P1, rep from * to last 1 (2: 3: 4: 5: 6) sts, K1 (2: 3: 4: 5: 6).
Row 6: P5 (6: 7: 0: 1: 2), K1, *P7, K1, rep from * to last 5 (6: 7: 0: 1: 2) sts, P5 (6: 7: 0: 1: 2).
Row 7: K4 (5: 0: 0: 0: 1), P1 (1: 0: 0: 1: 1), K1 (1: 0: 1: 1: 1), *P1, K5, P1, K1, rep from * to last 5 (6: 7: 0: 1: 2) sts, P1 (1: 1: 0: 1: 1), K4 (5: 5: 0: 0: 1), P0 (0: 1: 0: 0: 0).
Row 8: P3 (0: 1: 2: 3: 0), K1, *P3, K1, rep from * to last 3 (0: 1: 2: 3: 0) sts, P3 (0: 1: 2: 3: 0).
Row 9: K0 (1: 2: 3: 4: 5), *P1, K1, P1, K5, rep from * to last 3 (4: 5: 6: 7: 0) sts, P1 (1: 1: 1: 1: 0), K1 (1: 1: 1: 1: 0), P1 (1: 1: 1: 1: 0), K0 (1: 2: 3: 4: 5).
Row 10: P1 (2: 3: 4: 5: 6), K1, *P7, K1, rep from * to last 1 (2: 3: 4: 5: 6) sts, P1 (2: 3: 4: 5: 6).
These 10 rows complete border.
Beg with a K row, cont in st st as folls:
Work 2 (2: 4: 2: 2: 2) rows, ending with a WS row.
Next row (RS): K3, M1, K to last 3 sts, M1, K3.
Working all sleeve increases as set by last row, inc 1 st at each end of 14th (12th: 14th: 12th: 12th: 12th) and every foll 14th (12th: 14th: 12th: 14th: 12th) row to 55 (57: 55: 57: 55: 69) sts, then on every foll – (14th: 16th: 14th: 14th: -) row until there are - (59: 59: 63: 65: -) sts.
Cont straight until sleeve measures 46 (47: 48: 49: 50: 51) cm, ending with a WS row.
Shape top
Cast off 2 (3: 3: 4: 4: 5) sts at beg of next 2 rows. 51 (53: 53: 55: 57: 59) sts.
Dec 1 st at each end of next 3 rows, then on foll alt row, then on 4 foll 4th rows. 35 (37: 37: 39: 41: 43) sts.
Work 1 row.
Dec 1 st at each end of next and every foll alt row until 29 sts rem, then on foll 5 rows, ending with a WS row.
Cast off rem 19 sts.

MAKING UP
Press all pieces with a warm iron over a damp cloth.
Join right shoulder seam using back stitch or mattress stitch if preferred.

Neckband
With RS facing and using 4mm (US 6) needles, pick up and knit 15 (15: 15: 16: 16: 16) sts down left side of neck, 17 (19: 19: 19: 19: 19) sts from front, 15 (15: 15: 16: 16: 16) sts up right side of neck, then 32 (34: 34: 36: 36: 36) sts from back. 79 (83: 83: 87: 87: 87) sts.
Row 1 (WS): P3, *inc knitwise in next st, P3, rep from * to end. 98 (103: 103: 108: 108: 108) sts.
Row 2: *K3, P2, rep from * to last 3 sts, K3.
Row 3: P3, *K2, P3, rep from * to end.
Rep last 2 rows until neckband measures 2.5 cm, ending with a **RS** row.
Next row (WS): P3, *K2tog, P3, rep from * to end. 79 (83: 83: 87: 87: 87) sts.
Cast off in rib.
Join left shoulder and neckband seam.
Join side seams, leaving seams open for first 24 rows (for side seam openings).
Join sleeve seams. Insert sleeves into armholes.

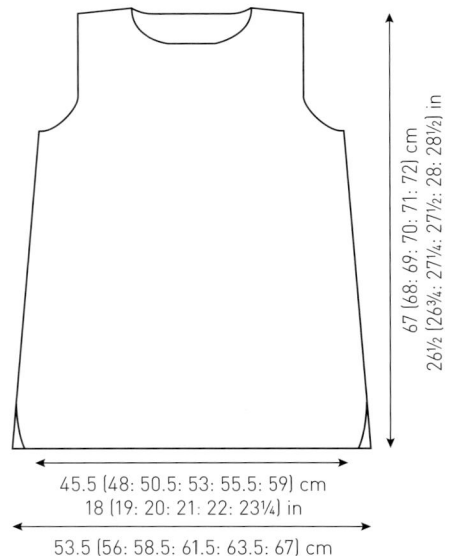

67 (68: 69: 70: 71: 72) cm
26½ (26¾: 27¼: 27½: 28: 28½) in

45.5 (48: 50.5: 53: 55.5: 59) cm
18 (19: 20: 21: 22: 23¼) in

53.5 (56: 58.5: 61.5: 63.5: 67) cm
21 (22: 23: 24: 25: 26½) in

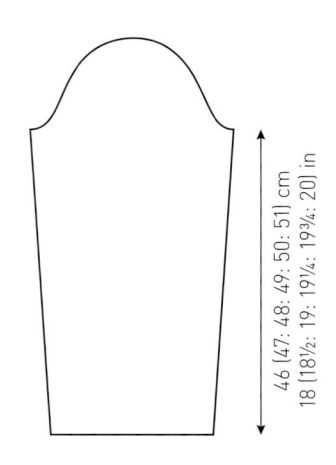

46 (47: 48: 49: 50: 51) cm
18 (18½: 19: 19¼: 19¾: 20) in

ISOLDE
Close-fitting ribbed wrap

Recommendation
Suitable for the novice knitter
Please see pages 36 & 37 for photographs.

	XS	S	M-L	XL	XXL	
To fit bust	81	86	91-97	102	109	cm
	32	34	36-38	40	43	in

Rowan Lima
| | 5 | 5 | 6 | 6 | 7 | x 50gm |

Photographed in Andes

Needles
1 pair 4mm (no 8) (US 6) needles
1 pair 4½mm (no 7) (US 7) needles

Tension
23 sts and 32 rows to 10 cm measured over rib using 4½mm (US 7) needles.

BACK and FRONT (both alike)
Cast on 105 (111: 117: 123: 129: 137) sts using 4½mm (US 7) needles.
Row 1 (RS): P1 (0: 0: 0: 0: 0), K3 (2: 0: 3: 1: 0), *P2, K3, rep from * to last 1 (4: 2: 0: 3: 2) sts, P1 (2: 2: 0: 2: 2), K0 (2: 0: 0: 1: 0).
Row 2: K1 (0: 0: 0: 0: 0), P3 (2: 0: 3: 1: 0), *K2, P3, rep from * to last 1 (4: 2: 0: 3: 2) sts, K1 (2: 2: 0: 2: 2), P0 (2: 0: 0: 1: 0).
These 2 rows form rib.
Cont in rib until work measures 14 (15: 15: 16: 17: 18) cm, ending with a WS row.
Shape shoulder darts
Counting in from both ends of last row, place markers after 9th (12th: 15th: 13th: 16th: 15th) sts in from both ends of row.
Next row (RS): Rib to marker, slip marker onto right needle, P2tog, rib to within 2 sts of next marker, P2tog tbl, slip marker onto right needle, rib to end.
Working all decreases as set by last row, dec 1 st at each end of 8th and 2 foll 6th rows, then on 4 foll 4th rows.
89 (95: 101: 107: 113: 121) sts.
Work 3 rows, ending with a WS row.
Change to 4mm (US 6) needles.
Dec 1 st at each end of next and foll 4th row.
85 (91: 97: 103: 109: 117) sts.
Work 3 rows, ending with a WS row.
Now reverse position of rib for turn-back as folls:
Row 1 (RS): K1 (0: 0: 0: 0: 0), P3 (2: 0: 3: 1: 0), *K2, P3, rep from * to last 1 (4: 2: 0: 3: 2) sts, K1 (2: 2: 0: 2: 2), P0 (2: 0: 0: 1: 0).
Row 2: P1 (0: 0: 0: 0: 0), K3 (2: 0: 3: 1: 0), *P2, K3, rep from * to last 1 (4: 2: 0: 3: 2) sts, P1 (2: 2: 0: 2: 2), K0 (2: 0: 0: 1: 0).
These 2 rows form rib for rest of wrap.
Work 4 rows, ending with a WS row.
Change to 4½mm (US 7) needles.
Work 3 rows, ending with a RS row.
Move markers one st further away from ends of rows, so there are now 10 (13: 16: 14: 17: 16) sts beyond markers at each end of row.
Next row (WS of main section, RS of turn-back): Rib to marker, slip marker onto right needle, M1P, rib to next marker, M1P, slip marker onto right needle, rib to end.
Working all increases as set by last row, inc 1 st at each end of 6th and 3 foll 6th rows, taking inc sts into rib.
95 (101: 107: 113: 119: 127) sts.
Cont in rib until work measures 8.5 (9.5: 9.5: 10.5: 11.5: 12.5) cm **from first inc,** ending with a WS row.
Cast off in rib.

MAKING UP
Press all pieces with a warm iron over a damp cloth.
Join both side seams using back stitch or mattress stitch if preferred, reversing seam for last 11 (12: 12: 13: 14: 15) cm for turn-back.

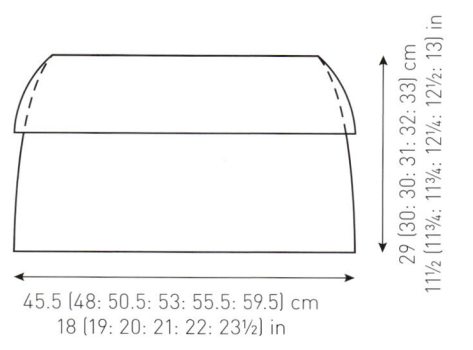

45.5 (48: 50.5: 53: 55.5: 59.5) cm
18 (19: 20: 21: 22: 23½) in

29 (30: 30: 31: 32: 33) cm
11½ (11¾: 11¾: 12¼: 12½: 13) in

ANNIS
Close-fitting sweater with buttoned neckline

Recommendation
Suitable for the knitter with a little experience
Please see pages 18 & 19 for photographs.

	XS	S	M	L	XL	XXL	
To fit bust	81	86	91	97	102	109	cm
	32	34	36	38	40	43	in

Rowan Angora Haze

        8   9   9   10   10   11 x 25gm
Photographed in Nest
OR
Rowan Pure Wool 4 ply
        8   8   9   10   10   11 x 50gm

Needles
1 pair 3mm (no 11) (US 2/3) needles
1 pair 3¼mm (no 10) (US 3) needles
2¾mm (no 12) (US 2) circular needle

Buttons – 6

Tension
Angora Haze: 28 sts and 38 rows to 10 cm measured over stocking stitch using 3¼mm (US 3) needles. 27 sts and 47 rows to 10 cm measured over garter stitch using 3mm (US 2/3) needles.
Pure Wool 4 ply: 28 sts and 38 rows to 10 cm measured over stocking stitch, 27 sts and 47 rows to 10 cm measured over garter stitch, both using 3¼mm (US 3) needles.

Special note:
Do **NOT** press Angora Haze. Pin the pieces out to size and steam.

BACK
Cast on 115 (121: 129: 135: 143: 153) sts using 3mm (US 2/3) needles.
Work in g st for 3 rows, ending with a **RS** row.
Row 4 (WS): K1, *P1, K1, rep from * to end.
Row 5: As row 4.
Last 2 rows form moss st.
Work in moss st for a further 19 rows, ending with a WS row.
Change to 3¼mm (US 3) needles.
Beg with a K row, now work in st st throughout as folls:
Work 2 rows, ending with a WS row.
Next row (RS): K9, K2tog, K to last 11 sts, K2tog tbl, K9.
Working all side seam decreases as set by last row, dec 1 st at each end of 8th and foll 8th row, then on 5 foll 6th rows.
99 (105: 113: 119: 127: 137) sts.
Work 13 (13: 15: 15: 15: 15) rows, ending with a WS row.
Next row (RS): K3, M1, K to last 3 sts, M1, K3.
Working all side seam increases as set by last row, inc 1 st at each end of 8th and 5 foll 8th rows, then on foll 10th row.
115 (121: 129: 135: 143: 153) sts.
Work 9 (9: 11: 11: 11: 11) rows, ending with a WS row.
Angora Haze version only
Change to 3mm (US 2/3) needles.
Both versions
Shape raglan armholes
Now working in g st throughout, cont as folls:
Cast off 8 sts at beg of next 2 rows.
99 (105: 113: 119: 127: 137) sts.**
Work 2 rows, ending with a WS row.
Next row (RS): K3, K2tog, K to last 5 sts, K2tog tbl, K3.
Working all raglan armhole decreases as set by last row, dec 1 st at each end of 4th and 7 (8: 5: 5: 5: 3) foll 4th rows, then on foll 0 (0: 7: 9: 11: 17) alt rows.
81 (85: 85: 87: 91: 93) sts.
Work 3 (3: 1: 1: 1: 1) rows, ending with a WS row.
Shape back neck
Next row (RS): K3, K2tog, K8 (9: 9: 9: 11: 11) and turn, leaving rem sts on a holder.
12 (13: 13: 13: 15: 15) sts.
Work each side of neck separately.
***Dec 1 st as before at raglan armhole edge of 4th (2nd: 2nd: 2nd: 2nd: 2nd) and foll 1 (2: 2: 2: 3: 3) alt rows **and at same time** dec 1 st at neck edge of next 4 rows, then on foll 1 (1: 1: 1: 2: 2) alt rows. 5 sts.
Work 1 row, ending with a WS row.
Next row (RS): K2, K3tog.
Next row: K3.
Next row: K3tog.
Next row: K1 and fasten off.***
With RS facing, rejoin yarn to rem sts, cast off centre 55 (57: 57: 59: 59: 61) sts, K to last 5 sts, K2tog tbl, K3.
12 (13: 13: 13: 15: 15) sts.
Complete to match first side, reversing shapings.

FRONT
Work as given for back to **.
Divide for front opening
Next row (RS): K46 (49: 53: 56: 60: 65) and turn, leaving rem sts on a holder.
Work each side of front opening separately.
Cast on 7 sts at beg of next row.
53 (56: 60: 63: 67: 72) sts.
Next row (RS): K3, K2tog, K to last 9 sts, K2tog tbl, yfwd (to make eyelet hole), K7.
Working all raglan armhole decreases as set by back raglan armhole and making eyelet holes (as set by last row) on every foll 4th row, cont as folls:
Dec 1 st at raglan armhole edge of 4th and 7 (8: 5: 5: 5: 3) foll 4th rows, then on foll 0 (0: 7: 9: 11: 17) alt rows.
44 (46: 46: 47: 49: 50) sts.
Work 3 (3: 1: 1: 1: 1) rows, ending with a WS row.
Shape front neck
Next row (RS): K3, K2tog, K8 (9: 9: 9: 11: 11) and turn, leaving rem 31 (32: 32: 33: 33: 34) sts on a holder.
12 (13: 13: 13: 15: 15) sts.
Work as given for back from *** to ***.
With RS facing, rejoin yarn to rem sts and K to end.
53 (56: 60: 63: 67: 72) sts.
Work 1 row.
Next row (RS): K7, yfwd, K2tog tbl (to make eyelet hole), K to last 5 sts, K2tog tbl, K3.
Work 3 rows.

Next row (buttonhole row) (RS): K2, K2tog, yfwd (to make a buttonhole), K3, yfwd, K2tog tbl (to make eyelet hole), K to last 5 sts, K2tog tbl, K3.

Working a further 4 buttonholes on every foll 7th (8th: 8th: 9th: 10th: 11th) row, complete to match first side, reversing shapings and working first row of neck shaping as folls:

Shape front neck
Next row (RS): Patt 31 (32: 32: 33: 33: 34) sts and slip these sts onto a holder, K to last 5 sts, K2tog tbl, K3.
12 (13: 13: 13: 15: 15) sts.
(**Note:** Make buttonholes on RS rows as given for first buttonhole, and, **for sizes XS, L and XXL,** make buttonholes on **WS** rows as folls: K to last 4 sts, yfwd, K2tog tbl – to make a buttonhole, K2.)

SLEEVES (both alike)
Cast on 55 (57: 59: 63: 65: 69) sts using 3mm (US 2/3) needles.
Work in g st for 3 rows, ending with a **RS** row.
Row 4 (WS): K1, *P1, K1, rep from * to end.
Row 5: As row 4.
Last 2 rows form moss st.
Work in moss st for a further 19 rows, inc 1 st at each end of 12th of these rows and ending with a WS row.
57 (59: 61: 65: 67: 71) sts.
Change to 3¼mm (US 3) needles.
Beg with a K row, now work in st st throughout as folls:
Work 4 rows, ending with a WS row.
Next row (RS): K3, M1, K to last 3 sts, M1, K3.
Working all sleeve increases as set by last row, inc 1 st at each end of 12th and every foll 12th row to 79 (77: 79: 79: 79: 79) sts, then on every foll 14th row until there are 81 (83: 85: 89: 91: 95) sts.
Cont straight until sleeve measures 46 (47: 47: 48: 49: 50) cm, ending with a WS row.

Angora Haze version only
Change to 3mm (US 2/3) needles.
Both versions
Shape raglan
Now working in g st throughout, cont as folls:
Cast off 8 sts at beg of next 2 rows.
65 (67: 69: 73: 75: 79) sts.
Working all raglan decreases in same way as back raglan armhole decreases, dec 1 st at each end of 5th and 4 (6: 6: 4: 7: 5) foll 6th rows, then on 5 (3: 3: 7: 4: 8) foll 4th rows.
45 (47: 49: 49: 51: 51) sts.
Work 1 row, ending with a WS row.
Cast off.

MAKING UP
Press all pieces with a warm iron over a damp cloth. (See special note)
Join all raglan armhole seams using back stitch or mattress stitch if preferred.

Neckband
With RS facing and using 2¾mm (US 2) circular needle, slip 31 (32: 32: 33: 33: 34) sts on right front holder onto right needle, rejoin yarn and pick up and knit 9 (9: 9: 9: 11: 11) sts up right side of front neck, place first marker on right needle, pick up and knit 44 (46: 48: 48: 50: 50) sts from top of right sleeve placing 2nd marker between centre 2 sts, place 3rd marker on right needle, pick up and knit 9 (9: 9: 9: 11: 11) sts down right side of back neck, 55 (57: 57: 59: 59: 61) sts from back, and 9 (9: 9: 9: 11: 11) sts up left side of back neck, place 4th marker on right needle, pick up and knit 44 (46: 48: 48: 50: 50) sts from top of left sleeve placing 5th marker between centre 2 sts, place 6th marker on right needle, pick up and knit 9 (9: 9: 9: 11: 11) sts down left side of front neck, then patt across 31 (32: 32: 33: 33: 34) sts on left front holder.
241 (249: 253: 257: 269: 273) sts.
Row 1 and every foll alt row: Knit.
Row 2 (RS): *K to within 4 sts of marker, K2tog tbl, K4 (marker is between centre 2 sts of these 4 sts), K2tog, rep from * 5 times more, K to end.
229 (237: 241: 245: 257: 261) sts.
Row 4: K2, K2tog, yfwd (to make 6th buttonhole), K3, yfwd, K2tog tbl (to make eyelet), K to last 9 sts, K2tog, yfwd (to make eyelet), K7.
Row 6: As row 2.
217 (225: 229: 233: 245: 249) sts.
Row 8: K7, yfwd, K2tog tbl (to make eyelet), K to last 9 sts, K2tog, yfwd (to make eyelet), K7.
Row 10: As row 2.
Cast off rem 205 (213: 217: 221: 233: 237) sts knitwise (on **WS**).
At base of front opening, neatly sew 7 cast-on sts in place behind right front opening edge. Join side and sleeve seams. Sew on buttons.

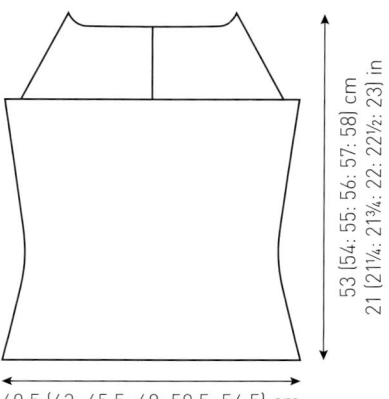

53 [54: 55: 56: 57: 58] cm
21 [21¼: 21¾: 22: 22½: 23] in

40.5 [43: 45.5: 48: 50.5: 54.5] cm
16 [17: 18: 19: 20: 21½] in

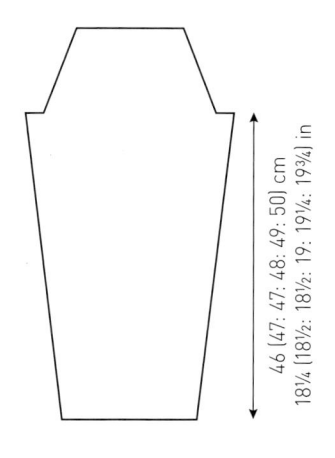

46 [47: 47: 48: 49: 50] cm
18¼ [18½: 18½: 19: 19¼: 19¾] in

STOMP
Boxy textured jacket with cosy collar

Recommendation
Suitable for the knitter with a little experience
Please see pages 20 & 21 for photographs.

	XS	S	M	L	XL	XXL	
To fit bust	81	86	91	97	102	109	cm
	32	34	36	38	40	43	in

Rowan Big Wool
8 8 9 9 10 11x 100gm
Photographed in Glum

Needles
1 pair 8mm (no 0) (US 11) needles
1 pair 9mm (no 00) (US 13) needles

Buttons – 6

Tension
12 sts and 12 rows to 10 cm measured over pattern using 9mm (US 13) needles.

Special abbreviation
inc 2 = increase 2 sts as folls: pick up loop lying between needles and work (P1, K1) into back of this loop.

BACK
Cast on 53 (55: 59: 61: 65: 69) sts using 8mm (US 11) needles.
Row 1 (RS): (K1 tbl) 1 (0: 0: 1: 1: 1) times, *P1 tbl, K1 tbl, rep from * to last 0 (1: 1: 0: 0: 0) st, (P1 tbl) 1 (0: 0: 1: 1: 1) times.
Row 2: (P1 tbl) 1 (0: 0: 1: 1: 1) times, *K1 tbl, P1 tbl, rep from * to last 0 (1: 1: 0: 0: 0) st, (K1 tbl) 1 (0: 0: 1: 1: 1) times.
These 2 rows form twisted rib.
Work in twisted rib for a further 8 rows, ending with a WS row.
Change to 9mm (US 13) needles.
Now work in patt as folls:
Row 1 (RS): K0 (1: 3: 0: 2: 0), place marker on needle, K2tog, *(K1, yfwd, K1) all into next st, sl 1, K2tog, psso, rep from * to last 3 (4: 6: 3: 5: 3) sts, (K1, yfwd, K1) all into next st, sl 1, K1, psso, place marker on needle, K0 (1: 3: 0: 2: 0).
Row 2: Purl, slipping markers from left needle to right needle.
These 2 rows form patt.
Cont in patt until back measures 24 (24: 25: 25: 25: 25) cm, ending with a WS row.
(**Note:** When working shaping through patt, move markers in by 4 sts as required and work sts beyond these markers in st st and sts between these markers in patt as set.)
Shape armholes
Keeping patt correct, cast off 3 sts at beg of next 2 rows. 47 (49: 53: 55: 59: 63) sts.
Dec 1 st at each end of next 3 (3: 3: 5: 5: 7) rows, then on foll 2 (2: 3: 2: 3: 2) alt rows. 37 (39: 41: 41: 43: 45) sts.
Cont straight until armhole measures 18 (19: 19: 20: 21: 22) cm, ending with a WS row.
Shape shoulders and back neck
Cast off 4 (4: 4: 4: 4: 5) sts at beg of next 2 rows. 29 (31: 33: 33: 35: 35) sts.
Next row (RS): Cast off 4 (4: 4: 4: 4: 5) sts, patt until there are 6 (7: 8: 7: 8: 7) sts on right needle and turn, leaving rem sts on a holder.
Work each side of neck separately.
Cast off 3 sts at beg of next row.
Cast off rem 3 (4: 5: 4: 5: 4) sts.
With RS facing, rejoin yarn to rem sts, cast off centre 9 (9: 9: 11: 11: 11) sts, patt to end.
Complete to match first side, reversing shapings.

LEFT FRONT
Cast on 32 (33: 35: 36: 38: 40) sts using 8mm (US 11) needles.
Row 1 (RS): (K1 tbl) 1 (0: 0: 1: 1: 1) times, *P1 tbl, K1 tbl, rep from * to last st, K1.
Row 2: K1, P1 tbl, *K1 tbl, P1 tbl, rep from * to last 1 (0: 0: 1: 1: 1) st, (K1 tbl) 1 (0: 0: 1: 1: 1) times.
These 2 rows set the sts – front opening edge st worked as a K st on every row with all other sts in twisted rib.
Cont as set for a further 8 rows, ending with a WS row.
Change to 9mm (US 13) needles.
Now work in patt as folls:
Row 1 (RS): K0 (1: 3: 0: 2: 0), place marker on needle, K2tog, *(K1, yfwd, K1) all into next st, sl 1, K2tog, psso, rep from * to last 10 sts, (K1, yfwd, K1) all into next st, sl 1, K1, psso, place marker on needle, patt 7 sts.
Row 2: Patt 7 sts, P to end, slipping markers from left needle to right needle.
These 2 rows set the sts – front opening edge 7 sts still in rib as set and all other sts now in patt.
Cont in patt until left front matches back to start of armhole shaping, ending with a WS row.
Shape armhole
Keeping patt correct, cast off 3 sts at beg of next row. 29 (30: 32: 33: 35: 37) sts.
Work 1 row.
Dec 1 st at armhole edge of next 3 (3: 3: 5: 5: 7) rows, then on foll 2 (2: 3: 2: 3: 2) alt rows. 24 (25: 26: 26: 27: 28) sts.
Cont straight until 4 (4: 4: 6: 6: 6) rows less have been worked than on back to start of shoulder shaping, ending with a WS row.
Shape front neck
Next row (RS): Patt 14 (15: 16: 16: 17: 18) sts and turn, leaving rem 10 sts on a holder (for collar).
Keeping patt correct, dec 1 st at neck edge of next 2 rows, then on foll 0 (0: 0: 1: 1: 1) alt row. 12 (13: 14: 13: 14: 15) sts.
Work 1 row, ending with a WS row.
Shape shoulder
Cast off 4 (4: 4: 4: 4: 5) sts at beg of next and foll alt row and at same time dec 1 st at neck edge of first of these rows.

Work 1 row.
Cast off rem 3 (4: 5: 4: 5: 4) sts.
Mark positions for 6 buttons along left front opening edge – first to come level with row 3, last to come 2 cm above start of front neck shaping, and rem 4 buttons evenly spaced between.

RIGHT FRONT

Cast on 32 (33: 35: 36: 38: 40) sts using 8mm (US 11) needles.
Row 1 (RS): K1, K1 tbl, *P1 tbl, K1 tbl, rep from * to last 0 (1: 1: 0: 0: 0) st, (P1 tbl) 0 (1: 1: 0: 0: 0) times.
Row 2: (P1 tbl) 1 (0: 0: 1: 1: 1) times, *K1 tbl, P1 tbl, rep from * to last st, K1.
These 2 rows set the sts – front opening edge st worked as a K st on every row with all other sts in twisted rib.
Row 3 (buttonhole row) (RS): K1, K1 tbl, P2tog tbl, yrn (to make a buttonhole), rib to end.
Working a further 4 buttonholes in this way to correspond with positions marked for buttons on left front and noting that no further reference will be made to buttonholes, cont as folls:
Work 7 rows, ending with a WS row.
Change to 9mm (US 13) needles.
Now work in patt as folls:
Row 1 (RS): Patt 7 sts, place marker on needle, K2tog, *(K1, yfwd, K1) all into next st, sl 1, K2tog, psso, rep from * to last 3 (4: 6: 3: 5: 3) sts, (K1, yfwd, K1) all into next st, sl 1, K1, psso, place marker on needle, K0 (1: 3: 0: 2: 0).
Row 2: P to last 7 sts, patt 7 sts, slipping markers from left needle to right needle.
These 2 rows set the sts – front opening edge 7 sts still in rib as set and all other sts now in patt.
Complete to match left front, reversing shapings and working first row of neck shaping as folls:

Shape front neck
Next row (RS): Patt 10 sts and slip these sts onto a holder (for collar), patt to end.
14 (15: 16: 16: 17: 18) sts.

SLEEVES (both alike)

Cast on 27 (29: 31: 31: 33: 33) sts using 8mm (US 11) needles.
Row 1 (RS): (K1 tbl) 0 (1: 0: 0: 1: 1) times, *P1 tbl, K1 tbl, rep from * to last 1 (0: 1: 1: 0: 0) st, (P1 tbl) 1 (0: 1: 1: 0: 0) times.
Row 2: (P1 tbl) 0 (1: 0: 0: 1: 1) times, *K1 tbl, P1 tbl, rep from * to last 1 (0: 1: 1: 0: 0) st, (K1 tbl) 1 (0: 1: 1: 0: 0) times.

These 2 rows form twisted rib.
Work in twisted rib for a further 8 rows, ending with a WS row.
Change to 9mm (US 13) needles.
Now work in patt as folls:
Row 1 (RS): K3 (0: 1: 1: 2: 2), place marker on needle, K2tog, *(K1, yfwd, K1) all into next st, sl 1, K2tog, psso, rep from * to last 6 (3: 4: 4: 5: 5) sts, (K1, yfwd, K1) all into next st, sl 1, K1, psso, place marker on needle, K3 (0: 1: 1: 2: 2).
Row 2: Purl, slipping markers from left needle to right needle.
These 2 rows form patt.
(**Note**: When working shaping through patt, work increased sts in st st until there are sufficient to move markers out by 4 sts. Work sts beyond markers in st st and sts between these markers in patt as set.)
Cont in patt, shaping sides by inc 1 st at each end of next and every foll 8th (8th: 12th: 10th: 14th: 10th) row to 31 (33: 35: 41: 41: 39) sts, then on every foll 10th (10th: 14th: -: -: 12th) row until there are 37 (39: 39: -: -: 43) sts, taking inc sts into st st until there are sufficient to work in patt.
Cont straight until sleeve measures 46 (47: 48: 49: 50: 51) cm, ending with a WS row.

Shape top
Keeping patt correct, cast off 3 sts at beg of next 2 rows. 31 (33: 33: 35: 35: 37) sts.
Dec 1 st at each end of next and every foll alt row until 19 sts rem, then on foll 3 rows, ending with a WS row.
Cast off rem 13 sts.

MAKING UP

Press all pieces with a warm iron over a damp cloth.
Join both shoulder seams using back stitch or mattress stitch if preferred.

Collar
With RS facing and using 8mm (US 11) needles, slip 10 sts on right front holder onto right needle, rejoin yarn and pick up and knit 7 (7: 7: 9: 9: 9) sts up right side of neck, 15 (15: 15: 17: 17: 17) sts from back, and 7 (7: 7: 9: 9: 9) sts down left side of neck, then patt across 10 sts on left front holder.
49 (49: 49: 55: 55: 55) sts.
Keeping first and last sts of every row as K sts as set, now work all other sts in twisted rib as set by front opening edge sts and cont as folls:
Work 1 row, ending with a WS row.
Next row (buttonhole row) (RS): Rib 2, work 2 tog tbl, yrn (to make 6th buttonhole), rib to end.

Work a further 5 rows, ending with a WS row.
Next row (RS of body, WS of collar): Rib 16 (16: 16: 18: 18: 18), (inc 2, rib 4) twice, inc 2, rib 2 (2: 2: 4: 4: 4), (inc 2, rib 4) twice, inc 2, rib 15 (15: 15: 17: 17: 17).
61 (61: 61: 67: 67: 67) sts.
Change to 9mm (US 13) needles.
Cont in rib until collar measures 18 cm from pick-up row.
Cast off in rib.
Join side seams. Join sleeve seams.
Insert sleeves into armholes.
Sew on buttons.

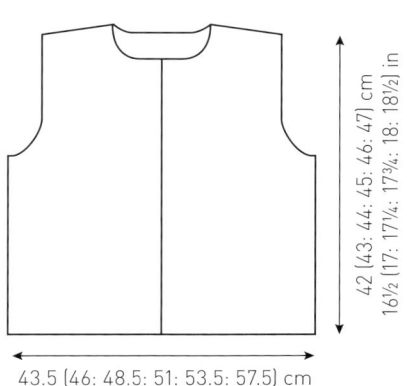

43.5 (46: 48.5: 51: 53.5: 57.5) cm
17 (18: 18: 20: 21: 22½) in

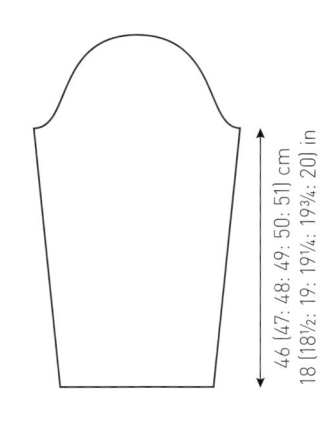

42 (43: 44: 45: 46: 47) cm
16½ (17: 17¼: 17¾: 18: 18½) in

46 (47: 48: 49: 50: 51) cm
18 (18½: 19: 19¼: 19¾: 20) in

WILDA
Midi length close-fitting aran dress

Recommendation
Suitable for the more experience knitter
Please see pages 22 & 23 for photographs.

	XS	S	M	L	XL	XXL	
To fit bust	**81**	**86**	**91**	**97**	**102**	**109**	**cm**
	32	34	36	38	40	43	in

Rowan Lima
17 18 18 19 19 20 x50gm
Photographed in Andes

Needles
1 pair 4mm (no 8) (US 6) needles
1 pair 4½mm (no 7) (US 7) needles
Cable needle

Tension
24 sts and 32 rows to 10 cm measured over double moss stitch using 4½mm (US 7) needles.

Special abbreviations
C2B = slip next st onto cn and leave at back of work, K1, then K1 from cn; **C2F** = slip next st onto cn and leave at front of work, K1, then K1 from cn; **C4B** = slip next 2 sts onto cn and leave at back of work, K2, then K2 from cn; **C4F** = slip next 2 sts onto cn and leave at front of work, K2, then K2 from cn; **C5B** = slip next 3 sts onto cn and leave at back of work, K2, slip centre st of this group of 5 sts back onto left needle and K this st, then K2 from cn; **C5F** = slip next 3 sts onto cn and leave at front of work, K2, slip centre st of this group of 5 sts back onto left needle and K this st, then K2 from cn; **cn** = cable needle; **Cr3L** = slip next 2 sts onto cn and leave at front of work, P1, then K2 from cn; **Cr3R** = slip next st onto cn and leave at back of work, K2, then P1 from cn.

BACK
Cast on 102 (108: 114: 120: 126: 136) sts using 4mm (US 6) needles.
Row 1 (RS): P0 (0: 1: 0: 0: 0), K1 (0: 2: 2: 1: 2), (P2, K2) 0 (1: 1: 2: 3: 4) times, P1, K2, *P1, K4, (P2, K2) twice, P1, (K2, P2) twice, K4, P1*, K2, P1, (K4, P2) 5 times, K4, P1, K2, rep from * to * once more, K2, P1, (K2, P2) 0 (1: 1: 2: 3: 4) times, K1 (0: 2: 2: 1: 2), P0 (0: 1: 0: 0: 0).
Row 2: K0 (0: 1: 0: 0: 0), P1 (0: 2: 2: 1: 2), (K2, P2) 0 (1: 1: 2: 3: 4) times, K1, P2, *K1, P4, (K2, P2) twice, K1, (P2, K2) twice, P4, K1*, P2, K1, (P4, K2) 5 times, P4, K1, P2, rep from * to * once more, P2, K1, (P2, K2) 0 (1: 1: 2: 3: 4) times, P1 (0: 2: 2: 1: 2), K0 (0: 1: 0: 0: 0).
Rows 3 and 4: As rows 1 and 2.
Row 5: P0 (0: 1: 0: 0: 0), K1 (0: 2: 2: 1: 2), (P2, K2) 0 (1: 1: 2: 3: 4) times, P1, K2, *P1, C4B, (P2, K2) twice, P1, (K2, P2) twice, C4F, P1*, K2, P1, (C4B, P2) 5 times, C4B, P1, K2, rep from * to * once more, K2, P1, (K2, P2) 0 (1: 1: 2: 3: 4) times, K1 (0: 2: 2: 1: 2), P0 (0: 1: 0: 0: 0).
Row 6: As row 2.
These 6 rows form fancy rib.
Work in fancy rib for a further 17 rows, ending with a **RS** row.
Row 24 (WS): Rib 33 (36: 39: 42: 45: 50), M1, rib 36, M1, rib 33 (36: 39: 42: 45: 50). 104 (110: 116: 122: 128: 138) sts.
Change to 4½mm (US 7) needles.
Beg and ending rows as indicated and repeating the 16, 18 and 20 row patt repeats throughout, now work in patt from chart as folls:
Inc 1 st at each end of 3rd and 3 foll 12th rows, then on 3 foll 14th rows, then on foll 16th row, taking inc sts into double moss st. 120 (126: 132: 138: 144: 154) sts.
Cont straight until back measures 49 (49: 50: 50: 50: 50) cm, ending with a WS row.
Keeping patt correct, dec 1 st at each end of next and 5 foll 6th rows, then on 2 foll 4th rows. 104 (110: 116: 122: 128: 138) sts.
Work 15 rows, ending with a WS row.
Inc 1 st at each end of next and 5 foll 6th rows, taking inc sts into double moss st. 116 (122: 128: 134: 140: 150) sts.
Cont straight until back measures 78 (78: 79: 79: 79: 79) cm, ending with a WS row.

Shape armholes
Keeping patt correct, cast off 3 (3: 4: 4: 5: 5) sts at beg of next 2 rows.
110 (116: 120: 126: 130: 140) sts.
Dec 1 st at each end of next 1 (3: 3: 5: 5: 7) rows, then on foll 1 (1: 2: 2: 3: 4) alt rows, then on foll 4th row. 104 (106: 108: 110: 112: 116) sts.
Cont straight until armhole measures 19 (20: 20: 21: 22: 23) cm, ending with a WS row.

Shape shoulders and back neck
Cast off 8 (8: 8: 8: 9: 9) sts at beg of next 2 rows. 88 (90: 92: 94: 94: 98) sts.
(**Note**: When casting off across top of cables, work 2 sts tog to reduce the chance of the shoulder edge stretching too much. St counts given relate to the original number of sts and do NOT take into account these decreases.)
Next row (RS): Cast off 8 (8: 8: 8: 9: 9) sts, patt until there are 12 (12: 13: 13: 12: 14) sts on right needle and turn, leaving rem sts on a holder.
Work each side of neck separately.
Cast off 4 sts at beg of next row.
Cast off rem 8 (8: 9: 9: 8: 10) sts.
With RS facing, rejoin yarn to rem sts, cast off centre 48 (50: 50: 52: 52: 52) sts, patt to end.
Complete to match first side, reversing shapings.

FRONT
Work as given for back until 20 (20: 20: 22: 22: 22) rows less have been worked than on back to start of shoulder shaping, ending with a WS row.

Shape front neck
Next row (RS): Patt 35 (35: 36: 37: 38: 40) sts and turn, leaving rem sts on a holder.
Work each side of neck separately.
Keeping patt correct, dec 1 st at neck edge of next 8 rows, then on foll 2 (2: 2: 3: 3: 3) alt rows, then on foll 4th row. 24 (24: 25: 25: 26: 28) sts.
Work 3 rows, ending with a WS row.

Shape shoulder
Cast off 8 (8: 8: 8: 9: 9) sts at beg of next and foll alt rows.
Work 1 row.
Cast off rem 8 (8: 9: 9: 8: 10) sts.
With RS facing, rejoin yarn to rem sts, cast off centre 34 (36: 36: 36: 36: 36) sts, patt to end.
Complete to match first side, reversing shapings.

SLEEVES (both alike)
Cast on 64 (66: 68: 72: 74: 78) sts using 4mm (US 6) needles.
Row 1 (RS): K1 (2: 3: 0: 1: 3), P2, *K3, P2, rep from * to last 1 (2: 3: 0: 1: 3) sts, K1 (2: 3: 0: 1: 3).
Row 2: P1 (2: 3: 0: 1: 3), K2, *P3, K2, rep from * to last 1 (2: 3: 0: 1: 3) sts, P1 (2: 3: 0: 1: 3).
These 2 rows form rib.
Work in rib for a further 21 rows, ending with a **RS** row.
Change to 4½mm (US 7) needles.

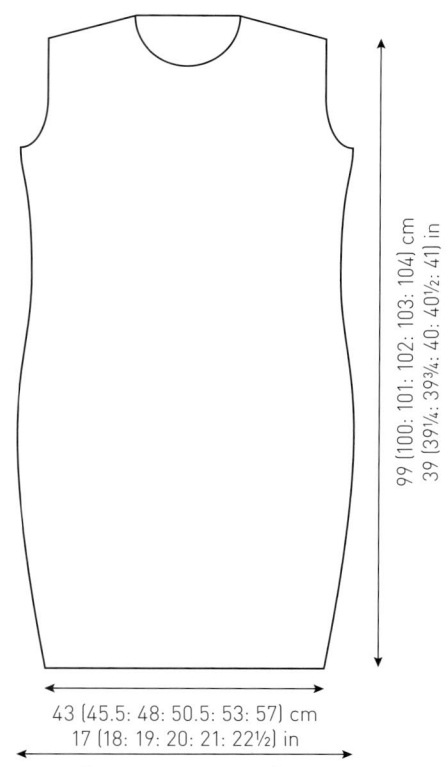

99 (100: 101: 102: 103: 104) cm
39 (39¼: 39¾: 40: 40½: 41) in

43 (45.5: 48: 50.5: 53: 57) cm
17 (18: 19: 20: 21: 22½) in

45 (47: 49.5: 52.5: 55: 59) cm
17¾ (18½: 19½: 19¾: 21¾: 23¼) in

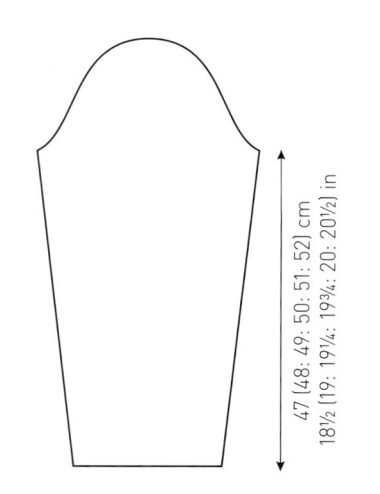

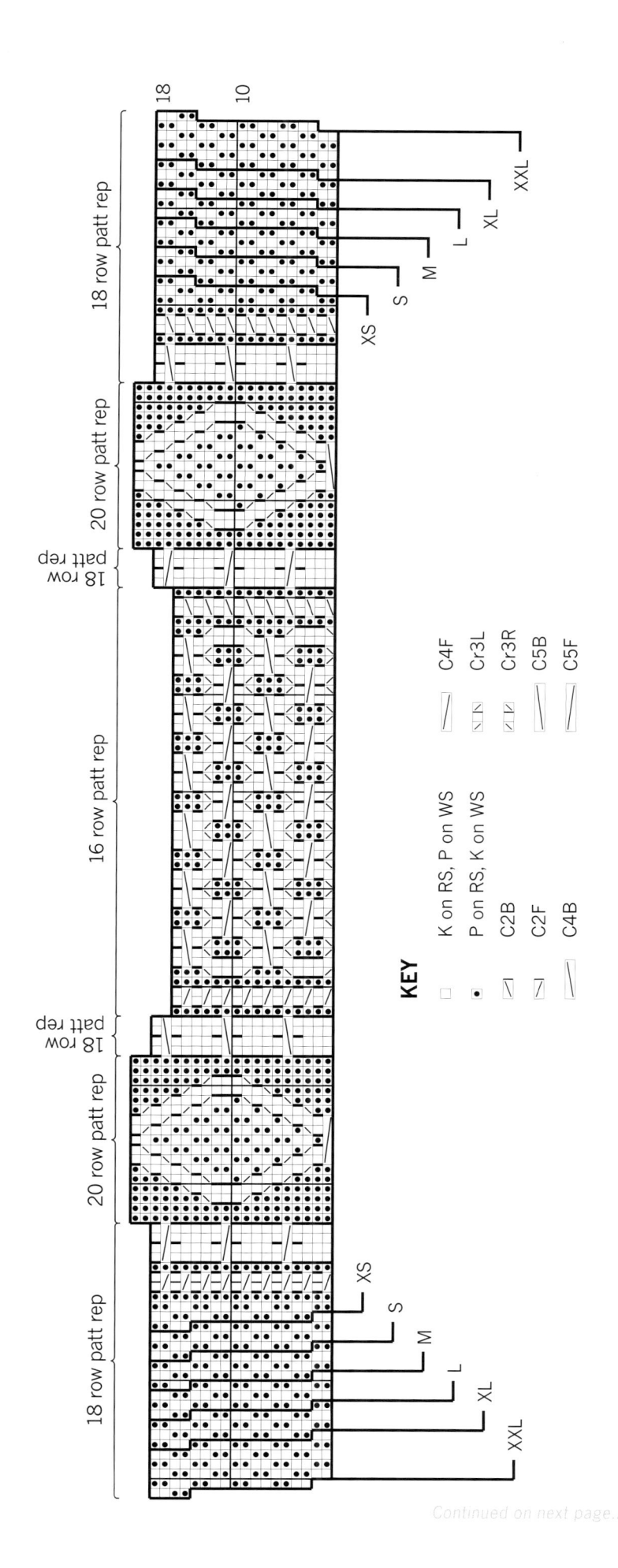

47 (48: 49: 50: 51: 52) cm
18½ (19: 19¼: 19¾: 20: 20½) in

KEY

□ K on RS, P on WS
• P on RS, K on WS
C2B
C2F
C4B
C4F
Cr3L
Cr3R
C5B
C5F

Continued on next page...

BRAM
Slouchy ribbed hat

Recommendation
Suitable for the novice knitter
Please see pages 22, 32 & 54 for photographs.

Rowan Angora Haze
Striped version
A Squeeze   3   x 25gm
B Love   1   x 25gm
Plain version
             3   x 25gm
Photographed in Tender & Caring

Needles
1 pair 3¾mm (no 9) (US 5) needles
1 pair 4½mm (no 7) (US 7) needles

Tension
24 sts and 30 rows to 10 cm measured over pattern using 4½mm (US 7) needles and yarn **DOUBLE**.

PLAIN HAT
Work as given for Striped Hat (below) but using same colour throughout.

STRIPED HAT (With pompom)
Cast on 107 sts using 4½mm (US 7) needles and yarn B **DOUBLE**.
Row 1 (RS): K3, *P1, K3, rep from * to end.
Row 2: K1, *P1, K3, rep from * to last 2 sts, P1, K1.
These 2 rows form patt.
Keeping patt correct, cont in stripes (using yarn **DOUBLE** throughout) as folls:
Rows 3 and 4: Using yarn B.
Rows 5 to 8: Using yarn A.
Rows 9 to 12: Using yarn B.
Rows 13 to 16: Using yarn A.
Rows 17 to 20: Using yarn B.
Break off yarn B and cont using yarn A **DOUBLE** only as folls:
Cont in patt until hat measures 10 cm, ending with a WS row.
Change to 3¾mm (US 5) needles.
Cont in patt until hat measures 18 cm, ending with a WS row.
Change to 4½mm (US 7) needles.
Cont in patt until hat measures 32 cm, ending with a WS row.

Shape top
Row 1 (RS): K1, *K1, P3tog, rep from * to last 2 sts, K2. 55 sts.
Row 2: K1, *P1, K1, rep from * to end.
Row 3: *K2tog, rep from * to last st, K1. 28 sts.
Row 4: P1, *P2tog, rep from * to last stitch, P1.
Break yarn and thread through rem 15 sts.
Pull up tight and fasten off securely.
Sew back seam, reversing seam for turn-back.
Using yarn B, make a 5 cm (2 in) diameter pompom and attach to top of hat.

WILDA – *Continued from previous page.*

Row 24 (WS): P1 (2: 3: 0: 1: 3), K2tog, *P3, K2tog, rep from * to last 1 (2: 3: 0: 1: 3) sts, P1 (2: 3: 0: 1: 3). 51 (53: 55: 57: 59: 63) sts.
Now work in double moss st as folls:
Row 1 (RS): K1, *P1, K1, rep from * to end.
Row 2: P1, *K1, P1, rep from * to end.
Row 3: Inc in first st, K1, *P1, K1, rep from * to last st, inc in last st. 53 (55: 57: 59: 61: 65) sts.
Row 4: As row 2.
These 4 rows form double moss st and beg sleeve shaping.
Cont in patt, inc 1 st at each end of 7th (9th: 9th: 9th: 9th: 9th) and every foll 8th (10th: 10th: 10th: 10th: 10th) row to 57 (77: 75: 75: 75: 75) sts, then on every foll 10th (-: 12th: 12th: 12th: 12th) row until there are 75 (-: 79: 81: 85: 87) sts, taking inc sts into double moss st.
Cont straight until sleeve measures 47 (48: 49: 50: 51: 52) cm, ending with a WS row.

Shape top
Keeping patt correct, cast off 3 (3: 4: 4: 5: 5) sts at beg of next 2 rows. 69 (71: 71: 73: 75: 77) sts.
Dec 1 st at each end of next 5 rows, then on foll alt row, then on 5 foll 4th rows. 47 (49: 49: 51: 53: 55) sts.
Work 1 row.
Dec 1 st at each end of next and every foll alt row until 41 sts rem, then on foll 9 rows, ending with a WS row.
Cast off rem 23 sts.

MAKING UP
Press all pieces with a warm iron over a damp cloth.
Join right shoulder seam using back stitch or mattress stitch if preferred.

Neckband
With RS facing and using 4mm (US 6) needles, pick up and knit 19 (19: 19: 20: 20: 20) sts down left side of neck, 23 (25: 25: 25: 25: 25) sts from front, 19 (19: 19: 20: 20: 20) sts up right side of neck, then 41 (43: 43: 45: 45: 45) sts from back.
102 (106: 106: 110: 110: 110) sts.
Row 1 (WS): P2, *inc knitwise in next st, P3, rep from * to end.
127 (132: 132: 137: 137: 137) sts.
Row 2: *K3, P2, rep from * to last 2 sts, K2.
Row 3: P2, *K2, P3, rep from * to end.
Rows 4 and 5: As rows 2 and 3.
Row 6: As row 2.
Row 7: P2, *K2tog, P3, rep from * to end.
102 (106: 106: 110: 110: 110) sts.
Cast off in rib.
Join left shoulder and neckband seam.
Join side seams. Join sleeve seams.
Insert sleeves into armholes.

THOR
Fairisle cardigan worked in monotone shades

Recommendation
Suitable for the knitter with a little experience
Please see pages 24 - 27 for photographs.

	XS	S	M	L	XL	XXL	
To fit bust	81	86	91	97	102	109	cm
	32	34	36	38	40	43	in

Rowan Alpaca Cotton
A	Storm	5	6	6	7	7	8	x 50gm
B	Thunder	2	2	2	3	3	3	x 50gm
C	Raindrop	1	1	1	1	1	2	x 50gm

Needles
1 pair 4½mm (no 7) (US 7) needles
1 pair 5mm (no 6) (US 8) needles

Buttons – 8

Tension
16 sts and 20 rows to 10 cm measured over plain stocking stitch, 18 sts and 20 rows to 10 cm measured over patterned stocking stitch, both using 5mm (US 8) needles.

BACK
Cast on 102 (106: 112: 116: 122: 128) sts using 4½mm (US 7) needles and yarn A.
Row 1 (RS): K0 (2: 0: 2: 0: 3), *P2, K3, rep from * to last 2 (4: 2: 4: 2: 5) sts, P2, K0 (2: 0: 2: 0: 3).
Row 2: P0 (2: 0: 2: 0: 3), *K2, P3, rep from * to last 2 (4: 2: 4: 2: 5) sts, K2, P0 (2: 0: 2: 0: 3).
These 2 rows form rib.
Work in rib for a further 11 rows, ending with a **RS** row.
Change to 5mm (US 8) needles.
Row 14 (WS): P0 (2: 0: 2: 0: 3), *K2tog, P3, rep from * to last 2 (4: 2: 4: 2: 5) sts, K2tog, P0 (2: 0: 2: 0: 3). 81 (85: 89: 93: 97: 103) sts.
Beg with a K row, work in st st until back measures 39 (39: 40: 40: 40: 40) cm, ending with a **RS** row.
Next row (WS): P4 (6: 6: 2: 4: 6), M1, *P8 (8: 7: 8: 8: 7), M1, rep from * to last 5 (7: 6: 3: 5: 6) sts, P5 (7: 6: 3: 5: 6). 91 (95: 101: 105: 109: 117) sts.
Beg and ending rows as indicated and using the **fairisle** technique as described on the information page, cont in patt from chart, which is worked entirely in st st beg with a K row, as folls:
Work 22 rows, ending with a WS row. (Back should measure 50 (50: 51: 51: 51: 51) cm.)

Shape armholes
Keeping patt correct, cast off 5 (5: 6: 6: 7: 7) sts at beg of next 2 rows.
81 (85: 89: 93: 95: 103) sts.
Dec 1 st at each end of next 3 (5: 5: 7: 7: 9) rows, then on foll 3 (2: 3: 2: 2: 3) alt rows, then on foll 4th row. 67 (69: 71: 73: 75: 77) sts.
Work 23 (25: 23: 25: 27: 25) rows, ending after chart row 60 (62: 62: 64: 66: 68) and with a WS row. (Armhole should measure 19 (20: 20: 21: 22: 23) cm.)

Shape shoulders and back neck
Cast off 7 (7: 8: 8: 8: 8) sts at beg of next 2 rows. 53 (55: 55: 57: 59: 61) sts.
Next row (RS): Cast off 7 (7: 8: 8: 8: 8) sts, patt until there are 12 (12: 11: 11: 12: 13) sts on right needle and turn, leaving rem sts on a holder.
Work each side of neck separately.
Cast off 4 sts at beg of next row.
Cast off rem 8 (8: 7: 7: 8: 9) sts.
With RS facing, rejoin yarns to rem sts, cast off centre 15 (17: 17: 19: 19: 19) sts, patt to end.
Complete to match first side, reversing shapings.

LEFT FRONT
Cast on 56 (58: 61: 63: 66: 69) sts using 4½mm (US 7) needles and yarn A.
Row 1 (RS): K0 (2: 0: 2: 0: 3), *P2, K3, rep from * to last 6 sts, K6.
Row 2: P9, *K2, P3, rep from * to last 2 (4: 2: 4: 2: 5) sts, K2, P0 (2: 0: 2: 0: 3).
Row 3: K0 (2: 0: 2: 0: 3), *P2, K3, rep from * to last 6 sts, P6.
Row 4: K6, P3, *K2, P3, rep from * to last 2 (4: 2: 4: 2: 5) sts, K2, P0 (2: 0: 2: 0: 3).
These 4 rows set the sts – front opening edge 6 sts in ridge patt with all other sts in rib.
Cont as set for a further 9 rows, ending with a **RS** row.
Change to 5mm (US 8) needles.
Row 14 (WS): P9, *K2tog, P3, rep from * to last 2 (4: 2: 4: 2: 5) sts, K2tog, P0 (2: 0: 2: 0: 3). 46 (48: 50: 52: 54: 57) sts.
Row 15 (RS): K to last 6 sts, patt 6 sts.
Row 16: Patt 6 sts, P to end.
These 2 rows set the sts – front opening edge 6 sts still in ridge patt with all other sts now in st st.
Cont as set until left front measures 39 (39: 40: 40: 40: 40) cm, ending with a **RS** row.
Next row (WS): Patt 6 sts, P4 (5: 2: 3: 4: 1), M1, *P8, M1, rep from * to last 4 (5: 2: 3: 4: 2) sts, P4 (5: 2: 3: 4: 2). 51 (53: 56: 58: 60: 64) sts.
Beg and ending rows as indicated and using the **fairisle** technique as described on the information page, cont in patt from chart, which is worked entirely in st st beg with a K row, placing chart as folls:
Next row (RS): Work first 45 (47: 50: 52: 54: 58) sts as chart, using yarn A patt rem 6 sts.
Next row: Using yarn A patt 6 sts, work rem 45 (47: 50: 52: 54: 58) sts as chart.
These 2 rows set the sts – front opening edge 6 sts still in ridge patt using yarn A and all other sts now in patt from chart.
Keeping sts correct as now set, cont as folls:
Work 4 rows, ending with a WS row.

Shape front slope
Next row (RS): Patt to last 8 sts, patt 2 tog tbl, patt 6 sts.
Working all front slope decreases as set by last row, dec 1 st at front slope edge of 4th and 2 foll 4th rows. 47 (49: 52: 54: 56: 60) sts.
Work 3 rows, ending with a WS row.

Key
- □ A
- ■ B
- × C

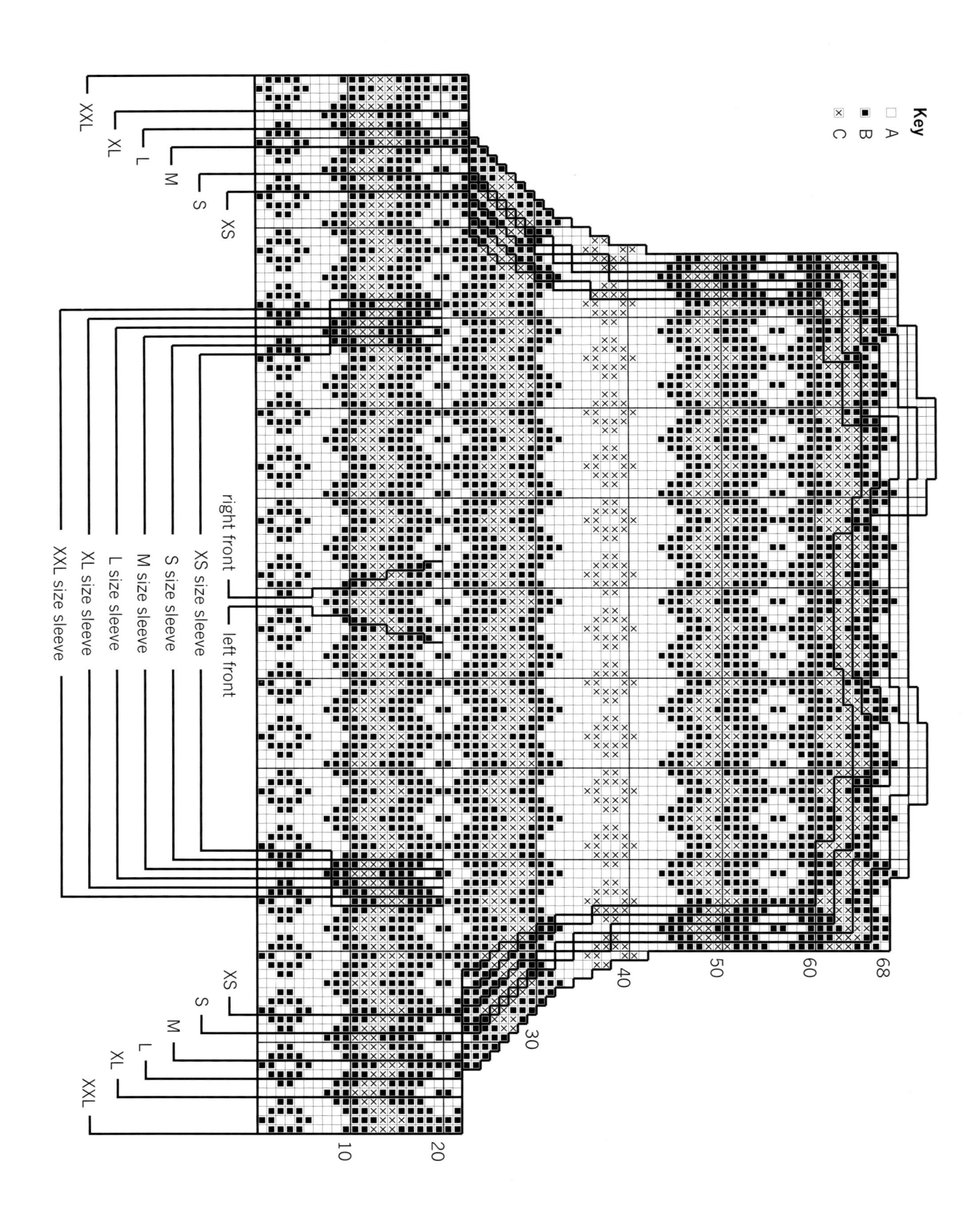

right front
left front

XS size sleeve
S size sleeve
M size sleeve
L size sleeve
XL size sleeve
XXL size sleeve

Shape armhole
Keeping patt correct, cast off 5 (5: 6: 6: 7: 7) sts at beg and dec 1 st at end of next row. 41 (43: 45: 47: 48: 52) sts.
Work 1 row.
Dec 1 st at armhole edge of next 3 (5: 5: 7: 7: 9) rows, then on foll 3 (2: 3: 2: 2: 3) alt rows, then on foll 4th row **and at same time** dec 1 st at front slope edge of 3rd and 0 (2: 2: 3: 3: 2) foll 4th rows, then on 1 (0: 0: 0: 0: 1) foll 6th rows. 32 (32: 33: 33: 34: 35) sts.
Dec 1 st at front slope edge **only** on 2nd (4th: 2nd: 4th: 6th: 4th) and 3 foll 6th rows.
28 (28: 29: 29: 30: 31) sts.
Work 3 rows, ending after chart row 60 (62: 62: 64: 66: 68) and with a WS row.
Shape shoulder
Cast off 7 (7: 8: 8: 8: 8) sts at beg of next and foll alt row, then 8 (8: 7: 7: 8: 9) sts at beg of foll alt row. 6 sts.
Inc 1 st at end of next row. 7 sts.
Cont in ridge patt using yarn A on these 7 sts only for a further 6.5 (7: 7: 7.5: 7.5: 7.5) cm (for back neck border extension), ending with a **RS** row.
Cast off in patt (on **WS**).
Mark positions for 8 buttons along left front opening edge – first button to come level with row 5, last button to come 2 cm below start of front slope shaping, and rem 6 buttons evenly spaced between.

RIGHT FRONT
Cast on 56 (58: 61: 63: 66: 69) sts using 4½mm (US 7) needles and yarn A.
Row 1 (RS): K9, *P2, K3, rep from * to last 2 (4: 2: 4: 2: 5) sts, P2, K0 (2: 0: 2: 0: 3).
Row 2: P0 (2: 0: 2: 0: 3), *K2, P3, rep from * to last 6 sts, P6.
Row 3: P6, K3, *P2, K3, rep from * to last 2 (4: 2: 4: 2: 5) sts, P2, K0 (2: 0: 2: 0: 3).
Row 4: P0 (2: 0: 2: 0: 3), *K2, P3, rep from * to last 6 sts, K6.
These 4 rows set the sts – front opening edge 6 sts in ridge patt with all other sts in rib.
Keeping sts correct as now set, cont as folls:
Row 5 (buttonhole row) (RS): Patt 2 sts, patt 2 tog tbl, yrn (to make a buttonhole), patt to end.
Working a further 7 buttonholes in this way to correspond with positions marked for buttons on left front and noting that no further reference will be made to buttonholes, cont as folls:
Work 8 rows, ending with a **RS** row.
Change to 5mm (US 8) needles.
Row 14 (WS): P0 (2: 0: 2: 0: 3), *K2tog, P3, rep from * to last 6 sts, P6.
46 (48: 50: 52: 54: 57) sts.
Row 15 (RS): Patt 6 sts, K to end.

Row 16: P to last 6 sts, patt 6 sts.
These 2 rows set the sts – front opening edge 6 sts still in ridge patt with all other sts now in st st.
Cont as set until right front measures 39 (39: 40: 40: 40: 40) cm, ending with a **RS** row.
Next row (WS): P4 (5: 2: 3: 4: 2), M1, *P8, M1, rep from * to last 10 (11: 8: 9: 10: 7) sts, P4 (5: 2: 3: 4: 1), patt 6 sts.
51 (53: 56: 58: 60: 64) sts.
Beg and ending rows as indicated and using the **fairisle** technique as described on the information page, cont in patt from chart, which is worked entirely in st st beg with a K row, placing chart as folls:
Next row (RS): Using yarn A patt 6 sts, work rem 45 (47: 50: 52: 54: 58) sts as chart.
Next row: Work first 45 (47: 50: 52: 54: 58) sts as chart, using yarn A patt rem 6 sts.
These 2 rows set the sts – front opening edge 6 sts still in ridge patt using yarn A and all other sts now in patt from chart.
Keeping sts correct as now set, cont as folls:
Work 4 rows, ending with a WS row.
Shape front slope
Next row (RS): Patt 6 sts, patt 2 tog, patt to end.
Working all front slope decreases as set by last row, complete to match left front, reversing shapings.

SLEEVES (both alike)
Cast on 49 (51: 53: 57: 57: 59) sts using 4½mm (US 7) needles and yarn A.
Row 1 (RS): K1 (2: 3: 0: 0: 1), *P2, K3, rep from * to last 3 (4: 5: 2: 2: 3) sts, P2, K1 (2: 3: 0: 0: 1).
Row 2: P1 (2: 3: 0: 0: 1), *K2, P3, rep from * to last 3 (4: 5: 2: 2: 3) sts, K2, P1 (2: 3: 0: 0: 1).
These 2 rows form rib.
Work in rib for a further 13 rows, ending with a **RS** row.
Change to 5mm (US 8) needles.
Row 16 (WS): P1 (2: 3: 0: 0: 1), *K2tog, P3, rep from * to last 3 (4: 5: 2: 2: 3) sts, K2tog, P1 (2: 3: 0: 0: 1). 39 (41: 43: 45: 45: 47) sts.
Beg with a K row, work in st st as folls:
Work 2 rows, ending with a WS row.
Next row (RS): K3, M1, K to last 3 sts, M1, K3.
Working all sleeve increases as set by last row, inc 1 st at each end of 10th (12th: 12th: 12th: 10th: 10th) and 0 (0: 0: 0: 2: 1) foll 10th rows, then on 4 (4: 4: 3: 3: 4) foll 12th rows, then on 0 (0: 0: 1: 0: 0) foll 14th row.
51 (53: 55: 57: 59: 61) sts.
Work 2 (2: 4: 4: 2: 2) rows, ending with a **RS** row.
Next row (WS): P7 (8: 8: 9: 10: 11), M1, *P12 (12: 13: 13: 13: 13), M1, rep from * to last 8 (9: 8: 9: 10: 11) sts, P8 (9: 8: 9: 10: 11).
55 (57: 59: 61: 63: 65) sts.

Beg and ending rows as indicated and using the **fairisle** technique as described on the information page, cont in patt from chart as folls:
Work 22 rows, inc 1 st at each end of 9th of these rows and ending with a WS row.
57 (59: 61: 63: 65: 67) sts. (Sleeve should measure 47 (48: 49: 50: 51: 52) cm.)
Shape armholes
Keeping patt correct, cast off 5 (5: 6: 6: 7: 7) sts at beg of next 2 rows. 47 (49: 49: 51: 51: 53) sts.
Dec 1 st at each end of next 3 rows, then on foll alt row, then on 3 foll 4th rows.
33 (35: 35: 37: 37: 39) sts.
Work 1 row.
Dec 1 st at each end of next and every foll alt row until 29 sts rem, then on foll 5 rows, ending with a WS row.
Cast off rem 19 sts.

MAKING UP
Press all pieces with a warm iron over a damp cloth.
Join both shoulder seams using back stitch or mattress stitch if preferred. Join cast-off ends of back neck border extensions, then sew one edge to back neck edge. Join side seams. Join sleeve seams. Insert sleeves into armholes. Sew on buttons.

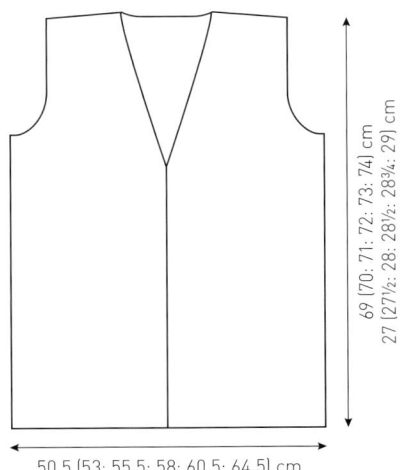

69 (70: 71: 72: 73: 74) cm
27 (27½: 28: 28½: 28¾: 29) cm

50.5 (53: 55.5: 58: 60.5: 64.5) cm
20 (21: 21¾: 22¾: 23¾: 25¼) in

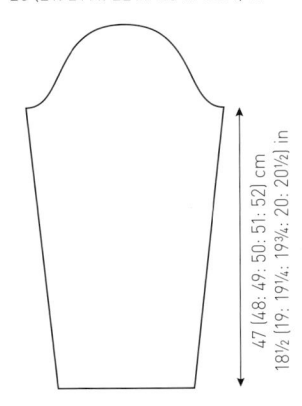

47 (48: 49: 50: 51: 52) cm
18½ (19: 19¼: 19¾: 20: 20½) in

FARA
Classic button through sweater

Recommendation
Suitable for the knitter with a little experience
Please see pages 28 & 29 for photographs.

	XS	S	M	L	XL	XXL	
To fit bust	81	86	91	97	102	109	cm
	32	34	36	38	40	43	in

Rowan Angora Haze
   8   9   9   10   10   11 x 25gm
Photographed in Squeeze
OR
Rowan Pure Wool 4 ply
   8   8   9   10   10   11 x 50gm

Needles
1 pair 2¾mm (no 12) (US 2) needles
1 pair 3¼mm (no 10) (US 3) needles

Buttons – 6

Tension
28 sts and 38 rows to 10 cm measured over stocking stitch using 3¼mm (US 3) needles.

Special note:
Do **NOT** press Angora Haze. Pin the pieces out to size and steam.

BACK
Cast on 143 (151: 161: 169: 179: 191) sts using 2¾mm (US 2) needles.
Row 1 (RS): K3 (2: 2: 1: 1: 2), P2, *K3, P2, rep from * to last 3 (2: 2: 1: 1: 2) sts, K3 (2: 2: 1: 1: 2).
Row 2: P3 (2: 2: 1: 1: 2), K2, *P3, K2, rep from * to last 3 (2: 2: 1: 1: 2) sts, P3 (2: 2: 1: 1: 2).
These 2 rows form rib.
Work in rib for a further 23 rows, ending with a **RS** row.
Change to 3¼mm (US 3) needles.
Row 26 (WS): P3 (2: 2: 1: 1: 2), K2tog, *P3, K2tog, rep from * to last 3 (2: 2: 1: 1: 2) sts, P3 (2: 2: 1: 1: 2).
115 (121: 129: 135: 143: 153) sts.
Beg with a K row, now work in st st throughout as folls:
Work 2 (2: 4: 4: 4: 4) rows, ending with a WS row.
Next row (RS): K4, K2tog, K to last 6 sts, K2tog tbl, K4.
Working all side seam decreases as set by last row, dec 1 st at each end of 10th and foll 10th row, then on 2 foll 8th rows.
105 (111: 119: 125: 133: 143) sts.
Work 19 (19: 21: 21: 21: 21) rows, ending with a WS row.
Next row (RS): K4, M1, K to last 4 sts, M1, K4.**
Working all side seam increases as set by last row, inc 1 st at each end of 12th and 3 foll 12th rows.
115 (121: 129: 135: 143: 153) sts.
Work 15 rows, ending with a WS row.
Shape armholes
Cast off 6 (6: 7: 7: 8: 8) sts at beg of next 2 rows.
103 (109: 115: 121: 127: 137) sts.
Dec 1 st at each end of next 5 (5: 7: 7: 9: 11) rows, then on foll 1 (3: 3: 4: 4: 5) alt rows, then on foll 4th row.
89 (91: 93: 97: 99: 103) sts.
Cont straight until armhole measures 18 (19: 19: 20: 21: 22) cm, ending with a WS row.
Shape shoulders and back neck
Next row (RS): Cast off 6 (6: 7: 7: 8: 9) sts, K until there are 11 (11: 11: 12: 12: 13) sts on right needle and turn, leaving rem sts on a holder.
Work each side of neck separately.
Cast off 4 sts at beg of next row.
Cast off rem 7 (7: 7: 8: 8: 9) sts.
With RS facing, rejoin yarn to rem sts, cast off centre 55 (57: 57: 59: 59: 59) sts, K to end.
Complete to match first side, reversing shapings.

FRONT
Work as given for back to **.
Work 1 row, ending with a WS row.
Divide for front opening
Next row (RS): K50 (53: 57: 60: 64: 69) and turn, leaving rem sts on a holder.
Work each side of front opening separately.
Next row (WS): Cast on 7 sts, work across these 7 sts as folls: K1, (P1, K1) 3 times, then P to end. 57 (60: 64: 67: 71: 76) sts.
Next row: K to last 6 sts, (P1, K1) 3 times.
Next row: K1, (P1, K1) 3 times, P to end.
Last 2 rows set the sts – front opening edge 7 sts in moss st with all other sts still in st st.
Keeping sts correct as now set, cont as folls:
Working all side seam increases as set by back, inc 1 st at beg of 7th and 3 foll 12th rows.
61 (64: 68: 71: 75: 80) sts.
Work 15 rows, ending with a WS row.
Shape armhole
Cast off 6 (6: 7: 7: 8: 8) sts at beg of next row.
55 (58: 61: 64: 67: 72) sts.
Work 1 row.
Dec 1 st at armhole edge of next 5 (5: 6: 6: 6: 6) rows. 50 (53: 55: 58: 61: 66) sts.
Work 1 (1: 0: 0: 0: 0) row, ending with a WS row.
Shape front neck
Next row (RS): K2tog, K31 (33: 35: 37: 40: 45) and turn, leaving rem 17 (18: 18: 19: 19: 19) sts on a holder (for neckband).
32 (34: 36: 38: 41: 46) sts.
Dec 1 st at neck edge of next 8 rows, then on foll 4 alt rows, then on foll 4th row, then on 3 foll 6th rows, then on foll 8th row, then on foll 10th row **and at same time** dec 1 st at armhole edge of 4th (2nd: 2nd: 2nd: next: next) and foll 0 (0: 0: 0: 1: 3) rows, then on foll 0 (1: 2: 3: 4: 5) alt rows, then on 0 (1: 1: 1: 1: 1) foll 4th row. 13 (13: 14: 15: 16: 18) sts.
Cont straight until front matches back to start of shoulder shaping, ending with a WS row.

Shape shoulder
Cast off 6 (6: 7: 7: 8: 9) sts at beg of next row.
Work 1 row.
Cast off rem 7 (7: 7: 8: 8: 9) sts.
Mark positions for 6 buttons along left front opening edge – first button to come in 13th row up from base of front opening, last button to come just above neck shaping, and rem 4 buttons evenly spaced between.
With RS facing, rejoin yarn to rem sts, (K1, P1) 3 times, K to end. 57 (60: 64: 67: 71: 76) sts.
Next row (WS): P to last 7 sts, K1, (P1, K1) 3 times.
Next row: (K1, P1) 3 times, K to end.
Last 2 rows set the sts – front opening edge 7 sts in moss st with all other sts still in st st.
Keeping sts correct as now set and working all side seam shaping as set by back, cont as folls:
Inc 1 st at end of 8th row.
58 (61: 65: 68: 72: 77) sts.
Work 1 row.
Next row (buttonhole row) (RS): K1, P1, K2tog, yfwd (to make a buttonhole), patt to end.
Working a further 4 buttonholes in this way to correspond with positions marked for buttons along left front opening edge and noting that no further reference will be made to buttonholes, cont as folls:
Inc 1 st at end of 10th and 2 foll 12th rows.
61 (64: 68: 71: 75: 80) sts.
Complete to match first side, reversing shapings and working first row of neck shaping as folls:

Shape front neck
Next row (RS): Patt 17 (18: 18: 19: 19: 19) sts and slip these sts onto a holder (for neckband), K to last 2 sts, K2tog.
32 (34: 36: 38: 41: 46) sts.

SLEEVES (both alike)
Cast on 77 (79: 81: 87: 89: 93) sts using 2¾mm (US 2) needles.
Row 1 (RS): K0 (1: 2: 0: 1: 3), P2, *K3, P2, rep from * to last 0 (1: 2: 0: 1: 3) sts, K0 (1: 2: 0: 1: 3).
Row 2: P0 (1: 2: 0: 1: 3), K2, *P3, K2, rep from * to last 0 (1: 2: 0: 1: 3) sts, P0 (1: 2: 0: 1: 3).
These 2 rows form rib.
Work in rib for a further 23 rows, ending with a RS row.
Change to 3¼mm (US 3) needles.
Row 26 (WS): P0 (1: 2: 0: 1: 3), K2tog, *P3, K2tog, rep from * to last 0 (1: 2: 0: 1: 3) sts, P0 (1: 2: 0: 1: 3). 61 (63: 65: 69: 71: 75) sts.
Beg with a K row, now work in st st throughout as folls:
Work 2 rows, ending with a WS row.
Next row (RS): K4, M1, K to last 4 sts, M1, K4.
Working all sleeve increases as set by last row, inc 1 st at each end of 12th (12th: 12th: 14th: 12th: 14th) and every foll 12th (12th: 12th: 14th: 12th: 14th) row to 85 (85: 83: 89: 81: 87) sts, then on every foll – (14th: 14th: 16th: 14th: 16th) row until there are - (87: 89: 91: 95: 97) sts.
Cont straight until sleeve measures 47 (48: 49: 50: 51: 52) cm, ending with a WS row.

Shape top
Cast off 6 (6: 7: 7: 8: 8) sts at beg of next 2 rows.
73 (75: 75: 77: 79: 81) sts.
Dec 1 st at each end of next 3 rows, then on foll alt row, then on 6 foll 4th rows.
53 (55: 55: 57: 59: 61) sts.
Work 1 row.
Dec 1 st at each end of next and every foll alt row until 43 sts rem, then on foll 7 rows, ending with a WS row. 29 sts.
Cast off 3 sts at beg of next 2 rows.
Cast off rem 23 sts.

MAKING UP
Press all pieces with a warm iron over a damp cloth. (See special note)
Join both shoulder seams using back stitch or mattress stitch if preferred.

Neckband
With RS facing and using 2¾mm (US 2) needles, slip 17 (18: 18: 19: 19: 19) sts on right front holder onto right needle, rejoin yarn and pick up and knit 45 (48: 48: 51: 54: 57) sts up right side of neck, 63 (65: 65: 67: 67: 67) sts from back, and 45 (48: 48: 51: 54: 57) sts down left side of neck, then patt across 17 (18: 18: 19: 19: 19) sts on left front holder.
187 (197: 197: 207: 213: 219) sts.
Working all sts in moss st as set by front opening edge sts, cont as folls:
Work 3 rows, ending with a WS row.
Next row (buttonhole row) (RS): K1, P1, K2tog, yfwd (to make 6th buttonhole), moss st to end.
Work in moss st for a further 3 rows, ending with a WS row.
Cast off in moss st.
At base of front opening, neatly sew 7 cast-on sts in place behind right front opening edge.
Join side seams. Join sleeve seams.
Insert sleeves into armholes.
Sew on buttons.

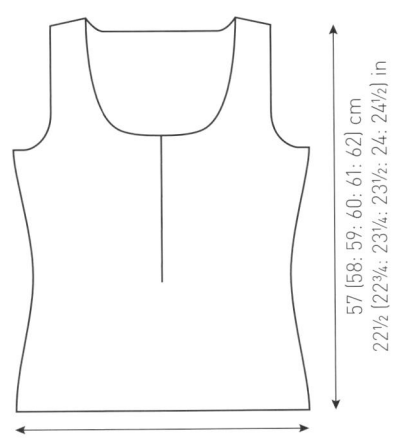

57 (58: 59: 60: 61: 62) cm
22½ (22¾: 23¼: 23½: 24: 24½) in

40.5 (43: 45.5: 48: 50.5: 54.5) cm
16 (17: 18: 19: 20: 21½) in

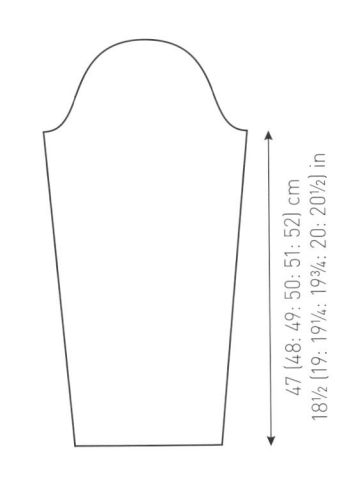

47 (48: 49: 50: 51: 52) cm
18½ (19: 19¼: 19¾: 20: 20½) in

DREW
Soft ribbed boyfriend cardigan

Recommendation
Suitable for the knitter with a little experience
Please see pages 30 & 31 for photographs.

	XS	S	M-L	L-XL	XXL	
To fit bust	81	86	91-97	97-102	109	cm
	32	34	36-38	38-40	43	in

Rowan Kid Classic and Kidsilk Haze
Kid Classic
    10   11   12   13   14 x 50gm
Kidsilk Haze
    7   7   8   8   9 x 25gm
Photographed in Kid Classic in Feather with Kidsilk Haze in Steel

Needles
1 pair 4mm (no 8) (US 6) needles
1 pair 5mm (no 6) (US 8) needles

Buttons – 6

Tension
21 sts and 28 rows to 10 cm measured over pattern using 5mm (US 8) needles and one strand each of Kid Classic and Kidsilk Haze held together.

Special note: We found it preferable to knit the two yarns together from separate balls rather than winding them together.

BACK
Cast on 103 (111: 119: 127: 135) sts using 4mm (US 6) needles and one strand each of Kid Classic and Kidsilk Haze held together.
Row 1 (RS): P1, *K1, P1, rep from * to end.
Row 2: K1, *P1, K1, rep from * to end.
These 2 rows form rib.
Work in rib for a further 22 rows, ending with a WS row.
Change to 5mm (US 8) needles.
Now work in patt as folls:
Row 1 (RS): K1, P1, *K3, P1, rep from * to last st, K1.
Row 2: K3, *P1, K3, rep from * to end.
These 2 rows form patt.
Cont in patt until back measures 46 (46: 47: 47: 47) cm, ending with a WS row.
Shape raglan armholes
Keeping patt correct, cast off 5 sts at beg of next 2 rows. 93 (101: 109: 117: 125) sts.
Size XS only
Work 2 rows.
Next row (RS): P1, K3, P2tog, patt to last 6 sts, P2tog tbl, K3, P1. 91 sts.
Next row: K2, P1, K2, patt to last 5 sts, K2, P1, K2.
Next row: P1, K3, P1, patt to last 5 sts, P1, K3, P1.
Next row: K2, P1, K2, patt to last 5 sts, K2, P1, K2.
Sizes M-L, L-XL and XXL only
Next row (RS): P1, K3, P2tog, patt to last 6 sts, P2tog tbl, K3, P1.
Next row: K2, P1, K1, K2tog tbl, patt to last 6 sts, K2tog, K1, P1, K2.
Rep last 2 rows – (-: 0: 2: 5) times more.
- (-: 105: 105: 101) sts.
All sizes
Next row (RS): P1, K3, P2tog, patt to last 6 sts, P2tog tbl, K3, P1.
Next row: K2, P1, K2, patt to last 5 sts, K2, P1, K2.
Rep last 2 rows 27 (31: 32: 32: 30) times more. 35 (37: 39: 39: 39) sts.
Next row (RS): P1, K3, P2tog, patt to last 6 sts, P2tog tbl, K3, P1.
Next row: K2, P1, K1, K2tog tbl, patt to last 6 sts, K2tog, K1, P1, K2.
Rep last 2 rows once more.
Cast off rem 27 (29: 31: 31: 31) sts.

POCKET LININGS (make 2)
Cast on 25 (25: 29: 29: 29) sts using 5mm (US 8) needles and one strand each of Kid Classic and Kidsilk Haze held together.
Work in patt as folls:
Row 1 (RS): P1, *K3, P1, rep from * to end.
Row 2: K2, *P1, K3, rep from * to last 3 sts, P1, K2.
These 2 rows form patt.
Work in patt for a further 38 rows, ending with a WS row.
Break yarn and leave sts on a holder.

LEFT FRONT
Cast on 59 (63: 67: 71: 75) sts using 4mm (US 6) needles and one strand each of Kid Classic and Kidsilk Haze held together.
Row 1 (RS): P1, *K1, P1, rep from * to last 6 sts, K6.
Row 2: K7, *P1, K1, rep from * to end.
These 2 rows set the sts – front opening edge 6 sts in g st with all other sts in rib.
Cont as set for a further 22 rows, ending with a WS row.
Change to 5mm (US 8) needles.
Now work in patt as folls:
Row 1 (RS): K1, P1, *K3, P1, rep from * to last 9 sts, K2, P1, K6.
Row 2: K7, *P1, K3, rep from * to end.
These 2 rows set the sts – front opening edge 6 sts still in g st, side edge sts in patt as given for back and 1 st in rev st st between.
Cont as set for a further 38 rows, ending with a WS row.
Place pocket
Next row (RS): Patt 9 (13: 13: 13: 17) sts, slip next 25 (25: 29: 29: 29) sts onto a holder and, in their place, patt across 25 (25: 29: 29: 29) sts of first pocket lining, patt 25 (25: 25: 29: 29) sts.
Cont straight until 18 rows less have been worked than on back to start of raglan armhole shaping, ending with a WS row.
Shape front slope
Next row (RS): Patt to last 8 sts, P2tog tbl, K6.
Working all front slope decreases as set by last row, dec 1 st at front slope edge of 4th and 3 foll 4th rows.
54 (58: 62: 66: 70) sts.
Work 1 row, ending with a WS row.

Shape raglan armhole
Keeping patt correct, cast off 5 sts at beg of next row. 49 (53: 57: 61: 65) sts.
Work 1 row, ending with a WS row.
Working all front slope decreases as now set and working all raglan armhole decreases as set by back, dec 1 st at raglan armhole edge of 3rd (next: next: next: next) and foll 0 (0: 2: 6: 12) rows, then on 1 (0: 0: 0: 0) foll 4th row, then on 21 (25: 26: 26: 24) foll alt rows **and at same time** dec 1 st at front slope edge of next and 11 (12: 13: 12: 11) foll 4th rows, then on 0 (0: 0: 1: 2) foll 6th rows. 14 sts.
Work 1 row, ending with a WS row.
Next row (RS): P1, K3, P2tog, P2tog tbl, K6. 12 sts.
Work 1 row.
Now working all decreases as set by front slope decreases, dec 1 st at front slope edge of next and foll 4 alt rows. 7 sts.
Working all sts in g st, cont on these 7 sts only for a further 12.5 (13: 13.5: 13.5: 13.5) cm (for back neck border extension), ending with a WS row.
Break yarn and leave these sts on a st holder.
Mark positions for 6 buttons along left front opening edge – first button to come level with row 5, last button to come 3 cm below start of front slope shaping, and rem 4 buttons evenly spaced between.

RIGHT FRONT
Cast on 59 (63: 67: 71: 75) sts using 4mm (US 6) needles and one strand each of Kid Classic and Kidsilk Haze held together.
Row 1 (RS): K6, P1, *K1, P1, rep from * to end.
Row 2: K1, *P1, K1, rep from * to last 6 sts, K6.
These 2 rows set the sts – front opening edge 6 sts in g st with all other sts in rib.
Work 2 rows, ending with a WS row.
Row 5 (buttonhole row) (RS): K2, K2tog tbl, yfwd (to make a buttonhole), patt to end.
Working a further 5 buttonholes in this way to correspond with positions marked for buttons on left front and noting that no further reference will be made to buttonholes, cont as folls:
Cont as set for a further 19 rows, ending with a WS row.
Change to 5mm (US 8) needles.
Now work in patt as folls:
Row 1 (RS): K6, P1, K2, P1, *K3, P1, rep from * to last st, K1.
Row 2: K3, *P1, K3, rep from * to last 8 sts, P1, K7.
These 2 rows set the sts – front opening edge 6 sts still in g st, side edge sts in patt as given for back and 1 st in rev st st between.
Cont as set for a further 38 rows, ending with a WS row.

Place pocket
Next row (RS): Patt 25 (25: 25: 29: 29) sts, slip next 25 (25: 29: 29: 29) sts onto a holder and, in their place, patt across 25 (25: 29: 29: 29) sts of second pocket lining, patt 9 (13: 13: 13: 17) sts.
Cont straight until 18 rows less have been worked than on back to start of raglan armhole shaping, ending with a WS row.
Shape front slope
Next row (RS): K6, P2tog, patt to end.
Working all front slope decreases as set by last row, complete to match left front, reversing shapings.

SLEEVES (both alike)
Cast on 51 (55: 55: 59: 59) sts using 4mm (US 6) needles and one strand each of Kid Classic and Kidsilk Haze held together.
Work in rib as given for back for 24 rows, ending with a WS row.
Change to 5mm (US 8) needles.
Now work in patt as given for back and cont as folls:
Work 2 rows, ending with a WS row.
Next row (RS): Patt 5 sts, M1, patt to last 5 sts, M1, patt 5 sts.
Working all sleeve increases as set by last row, keeping edge 5 sts correct in patt as set and taking inc sts into patt between inc sts, inc 1 st at each end of 4th and 6 (5: 4: 3: 2) foll 4th rows, then on 12 (13: 14: 15: 16) foll 6th rows. 91 (95: 95: 99: 99) sts.
Cont straight until sleeve measures 48 (49: 50: 51: 52) cm, ending with a WS row.
Shape raglan
Keeping patt correct, cast off 5 sts at beg of next 2 rows. 81 (85: 85: 89: 89) sts.
Working all raglan decreases in same way as back raglan armhole decreases, dec 1 st at each end of 3rd (next: 3rd: 3rd: 3rd) and 0 (0: 1: 1: 2) foll 4th rows, then on every foll alt row until 21 sts rem.
Work 1 row, ending with a WS row.
Keeping all raglan decreases correct as set, cont as folls:
Left sleeve only
Dec 1 st at each end of next row. 19 sts.
Cast off 5 sts at beg and dec 1 st at end of next row. 13 sts.
Dec 1 st at beg of next row. 12 sts.
Cast off 6 sts at beg of next row.
Right sleeve only
Cast off 6 sts at beg and dec 1 st at end of next row. 14 sts.
Dec 1 st at beg of next row. 13 sts.
Cast off 5 sts at beg and dec 1 st at end of next row. 7 sts.
Dec 1 st at beg of next row.

Both sleeves
Cast off rem 6 sts.

MAKING UP
Press all pieces with a warm iron over a damp cloth.
Join all raglan seams. Graft sts on holders at ends of back neck border extensions together, then sew one edge to back neck edge.
Pocket tops (both alike)
Slip 25 (25: 29: 29: 29) pocket sts onto 4mm (US 6) needles and rejoin one strand each of Kid Classic and Kidsilk Haze held together with RS facing.
Beg with row 2 (so this first row starts with a K st), work in rib as given for back for 6 rows, ending with a WS row.
Cast off in rib.
Sew pocket linings in place on inside, then neatly sew down ends of pocket tops.
Join side and sleeve seams.
Sew on buttons.

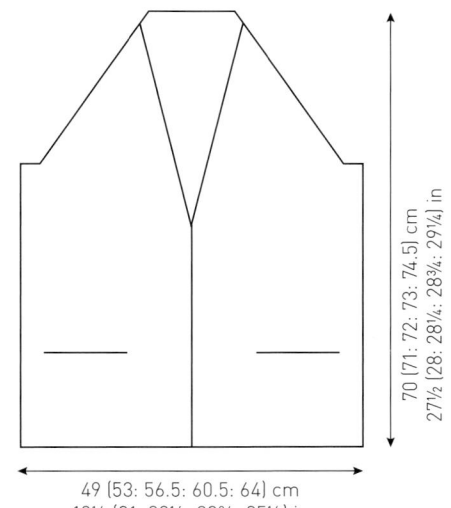

70 (71: 72: 73: 74.5) cm
27½ (28: 28¼: 28¾: 29¼) in

49 (53: 56.5: 60.5: 64) cm
19¼ (21: 22¼: 23¾: 25¼) in

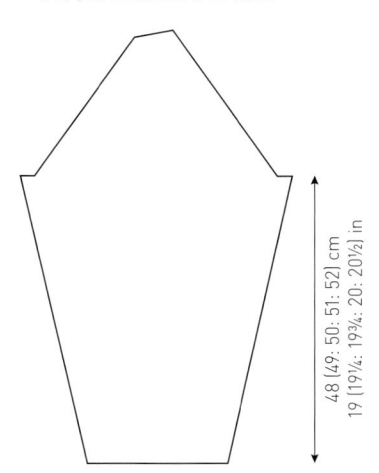

48 (49: 50: 51: 52) cm
19 (19¼: 19¾: 20: 20½) in

BLAIR
Classic V-neck sweater

Recommendation
Suitable for the knitter with a little experience
Please see pages 34 & 35 for photographs.

	XS	S	M	L	XL	XXL	
To fit bust	81	86	91	97	102	109	cm
	32	34	36	38	40	43	in

Rowan Angora Haze
10   11   12   12   13   14 x 25gm
Photographed in Caring

Needles
1 pair 2¾mm (no 12) (US 2) needles
1 pair 3¼mm (no 10) (US 3) needles

Tension
28 sts and 38 rows to 10 cm measured over stocking stitch using 3¼mm (US 3) needles.

BACK
Cast on 137 (143: 151: 157: 165: 175) sts using 2¾mm (US 2) needles.
Row 1 (RS): K1, *P1, K1, rep from * to end.
Row 2: P1, *K1, P1, rep from * to end.
These 2 rows form rib.
Cont in rib until back measures 8 cm, dec 1 st at centre of last row and ending with a WS row. 136 (142: 150: 156: 164: 174) sts.
Change to 3¼mm (US 3) needles.
Beg with a K row, now work in st st throughout as folls:
Cont straight until back measures 40 (40: 41: 41: 41: 41) cm, ending with a WS row.

Shape armholes
Cast off 4 (4: 5: 5: 6: 6) sts at beg of next 2 rows.
128 (134: 140: 146: 152: 162) sts.
Next row (RS): K3, K2tog, K to last 5 sts, K2tog tbl, K3.
Working all armhole decreases as set by last row, dec 1 st at each end of 2nd and foll 3 (4: 5: 6: 7: 8) alt rows, then on 6 (7: 8: 8: 9: 11) foll 4th rows.
106 (108: 110: 114: 116: 120) sts.
Cont straight until armhole measures 21 (22: 22: 23: 24: 26) cm, ending with a WS row.

Shape shoulders and back neck
Next row (RS): Cast off 6 (6: 7: 7: 8: 9) sts, K until there are 11 (11: 11: 12: 12: 13) sts on right needle and turn, leaving rem sts on a holder.
Work each side of neck separately.
Cast off 4 sts at beg of next row.
Cast off rem 7 (7: 7: 8: 8: 9) sts.
With RS facing, rejoin yarn to rem sts, cast off centre 72 (74: 74: 76: 76: 76) sts, K to end.
Complete to match first side, reversing shapings.

FRONT
Work as given for back until 2 rows less have been worked than on back to start of armhole shaping, ending with a WS row.

Divide for neck
Next row (RS): K65 (68: 72: 75: 79: 84), K2tog tbl, K1 and turn, leaving rem sts on a holder.
67 (70: 74: 77: 81: 86) sts.
Work each side of neck separately.
Work 1 row.

Shape armhole
Next row (RS): Cast off 4 (4: 5: 5: 6: 6) sts, K to last 3 sts, K2tog tbl, K1.
62 (65: 68: 71: 74: 79) sts.
Working all neck decreases as set by last row and all armhole decreases as set by back, cont as folls:
Work 1 row.
Dec 1 st at neck edge of next and foll 37 (37: 37: 37: 35: 33) alt rows, then on 0 (1: 1: 2: 4: 6) foll 4th rows **and at same time** dec 1 st at armhole edge of next and foll 4 (5: 6: 7: 8: 9) alt rows, then on 6 (7: 8: 8: 9: 11) foll 4th rows.
13 (13: 14: 15: 16: 18) sts.
Work a few rows straight until front matches back to start of shoulder shaping, ending with a WS row.

Shape shoulder
Cast off 6 (6: 7: 7: 8: 9) sts at beg of next row.
Work 1 row.
Cast off rem 7 (7: 7: 8: 8: 9) sts.
With RS facing, rejoin yarn to rem sts, K1, K2tog, K to end. 67 (70: 74: 77: 81: 86) sts.
Complete to match first side, reversing shapings.

SLEEVES (both alike)
Cast on 59 (61: 63: 67: 69: 73) sts using 2¾mm (US 2) needles.
Work in rib as given for back for 8 cm, ending with a WS row.
Change to 3¼mm (US 3) needles.
Beg with a K row, now work in st st throughout as folls:
Work 2 rows, ending with a WS row.
Next row (RS): K4, M1, K to last 4 sts, M1, K4.
Working all sleeve increases as set by last row, inc 1 st at each end of 8th (8th: 8th: 10th: 8th: 10th) and every foll 8th (8th: 8th: 10th: 8th: 10th) row to 81 (79: 77: 93: 77: 93) sts, then on every foll 10th (10th: 10th: 12th: 10th: 12th) row until there are 89 (91: 93: 95: 99: 101) sts.
Cont straight until sleeve measures 45 (46: 47: 48: 49: 50) cm, ending with a WS row.

Shape top
Cast off 4 (4: 5: 5: 6: 6) sts at beg of next 2 rows. 81 (83: 83: 85: 87: 89) sts.
Dec 1 st at each end of next 3 rows, then on every foll alt row until 35 sts rem, then on foll 3 rows, ending with a WS row.
Cast off rem 29 sts.

MAKING UP
Do NOT press. Pin pieces out to size and steam.
Join right shoulder seam using back stitch or mattress stitch if preferred.
Neckband
With RS facing and using 2¾mm (US 2) needles, pick up and knit 68 (72: 72: 76: 80: 84) sts down left side of neck, place marker on needle, pick up and knit 68 (72: 72: 76: 80: 84) sts up right side of neck, then 82 sts from back.
218 (226: 226: 234: 242: 250) sts.
Row 1 (WS): (K1, P1) 2 (0: 0: 2: 0: 2) times, *inc knitwise in next st, K1, P1, K1, inc purlwise in next st, P1, K1, P1, rep from * to within 2 sts of marker, P2tog, slip marker onto right needle, P2tog tbl, **P1, K1, P1, inc knitwise in next st, K1, P1, K1, inc purlwise in next st, rep from ** to last 2 (6: 6: 2: 6: 2) sts, (P1, K1) 1 (3: 3: 1: 3: 1) times.
268 (278: 278: 288: 298: 308) sts.
Row 2: *P1, K1, rep from * to within 3 sts of marker, P1, K2tog tbl, slip marker onto right needle, K2tog, **P1, K1, rep from ** to last st, P1.
This row sets position of rib as given for back. Keeping rib correct as now set, cont as folls:
Row 3: Rib to within 2 sts of marker, P2tog, slip marker onto right needle, P2tog tbl, rib to end.
Row 4: Rib to within 2 sts of marker, K2tog tbl, slip marker onto right needle, K2tog, rib to end.
Rows 5 and 6: As rows 3 and 4.
Row 7: As row 3.
256 (266: 266: 276: 286: 296) sts.
Now cast off in rib, decreasing every 5 sts by replacing (K1, P1) with (K2tog tbl) and replacing (P1, K1) with (K2tog).
(**Note**: after marker has been reached, mirror position of decreases on second side of neck.)
Join left shoulder and neckband seam.
oin side seams. Join sleeve seams.
Insert sleeves into armholes.

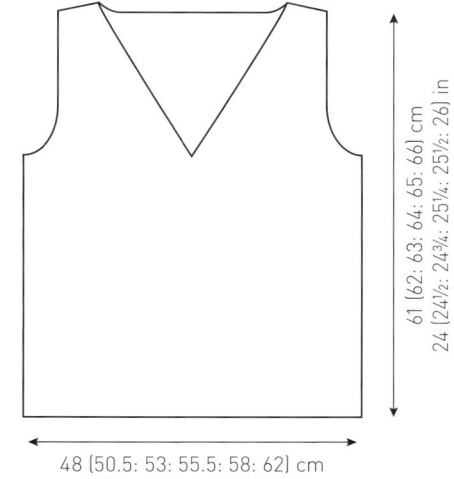

61 (62: 63: 64: 65: 66) cm
24 (24½: 24¾: 25¼: 25½: 26) in

48 (50.5: 53: 55.5: 58: 62) cm
19 (20: 21: 22: 23: 24½) in

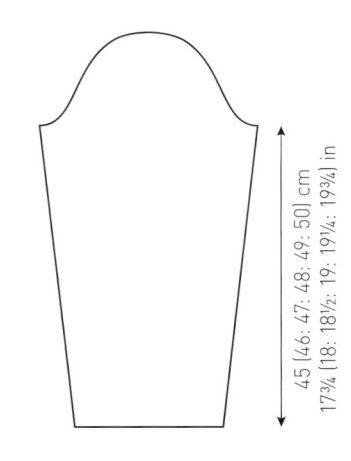

45 (46: 47: 48: 49: 50) cm
17¾ (18: 18½: 19: 19¼: 19¾) in

MYRA
Garter stitch cardigan with eyelet peplum

Recommendation
Suitable for the knitter with a little experience
Please see pages 39 - 41 for photographs.

	XS	S	M	L	XL	XXL	
To fit bust	81	86	91	97	102	109	cm
	32	34	36	38	40	43	in

Rowan Baby Alpaca DK
11 12 12 13 13 14 x 50gm
Photographed in Jacob

Needles
1 pair 3mm (no 11) (US 2/3) needles
1 pair 3¼mm (no 10) (US 3) needles

Buttons – 6

Tension
24 sts and 44 rows to 10 cm measured over garter stitch using 3¼mm (US 3) needles.

BACK
Hem border
Cast on 29 (29: 29: 31: 31: 31) sts using 3¼mm (US 3) needles.
Work in g st for 2 rows, ending with a WS row.
Now work in border patt as folls:
Rows 1 to 3: Knit.
Row 4 (WS): K2, *yrn, P2tog, rep from * to last st, K1.
Rows 5 to 9: Knit.
Row 10: K2, P to last 6 sts, wrap next st (by slipping next st from left needle onto right needle, taking yarn to opposite side of work between needles and then slipping same st back onto left needle - when working back across wrapped sts work the wrapped st and the wrapping loop tog as one st) and turn.
Row 11: K to end.
Row 12: Knit.
These 12 rows form border patt.
Cont in patt until hem border measures approx 33.5 (36: 38.5: 41: 43.5: 47.5) cm, ending after patt row 9 and with a **RS** row.
Cast off knitwise (on **WS**).

Main section
With RS facing and using 3¼mm (US 3) needles, pick up and knit 81 (87: 93: 99: 105: 115) sts evenly along shorter row-end edge of hem border.
Now work in g st throughout as folls:
Work 11 rows, ending with a WS row.
Next row (RS): K3, M1, K to last 3 sts, M1, K3.
Working all side seam increases as set by last row, inc 1 st at each end of 10th and 5 foll 12th rows. 95 (101: 107: 113: 119: 129) sts.
Work 11 rows, ending with a WS row.

Shape armholes
Cast off 4 (4: 5: 5: 6: 6) sts at beg of next 2 rows. 87 (93: 97: 103: 107: 117) sts.
Dec 1 st at each end of next 1 (3: 3: 5: 5: 7) rows, then on foll 3 (3: 4: 4: 5: 6) alt rows, then on 2 foll 4th rows.
75 (77: 79: 81: 83: 87) sts.
Cont straight until armhole measures 16 (17: 17: 18: 19: 20) cm, ending with a WS row.

Shape back neck
Next row (RS): K21 (21: 22: 22: 23: 25) and turn, leaving rem sts on a holder.
Work each side of neck separately.
Work 1 row.
Next row (RS): K to last 5 sts, K2tog tbl, K3.
20 (20: 21: 21: 22: 24) sts.
Work 1 row.

Shape shoulder
Next row (RS): Cast off 6 (6: 7: 7: 7: 8) sts, K until there are 9 (9: 9: 9: 10: 11) sts on right needle, K2tog tbl, K3.
Work 1 row.
Cast off 6 (6: 7: 7: 7: 8) sts at beg of next row.
Work 1 row.
Cast off rem 7 (7: 6: 6: 7: 7) sts.
With RS facing, rejoin yarn to rem sts, cast off centre 33 (35: 35: 37: 37: 37) sts, K to end.
Complete to match first side, reversing shapings.

LEFT FRONT
Hem border
Cast on 29 (29: 29: 31: 31: 31) sts using 3¼mm (US 3) needles.
Work in g st for 2 rows, ending with a WS row.
Now work in border patt as given for back until this border measures approx 20 (21.5: 22.5: 24: 25: 27) cm, ending after patt row 9 and with a RS row.
Work in g st for 2 rows, ending with a **RS** row.
Cast off knitwise (on **WS**).

Main section
With RS facing and using 3¼mm (US 3) needles, pick up and knit 48 (51: 54: 57: 60: 65) sts evenly along shorter row-end edge of hem border.
Now work in g st throughout as folls:
Work 11 rows, ending with a WS row.
Working all side seam increases as set by back, inc 1 st at beg of next and foll 10th row, then on 5 foll 12th rows.
55 (58: 61: 64: 67: 72) sts.
Work 11 rows, ending with a WS row.

Shape armhole
Cast off 4 (4: 5: 5: 6: 6) sts at beg of next row.
51 (54: 56: 59: 61: 66) sts.
Work 1 row.
Dec 1 st at armhole edge of next 1 (3: 3: 5: 5: 7) rows, then on foll 3 (3: 4: 4: 5: 6) alt rows, then on 2 foll 4th rows.
45 (46: 47: 48: 49: 51) sts.
Cont straight until 21 (21: 21: 25: 25: 25) rows less have been worked than on back to start of shoulder shaping, ending with a RS row.

Shape front neck
Cast off 14 (15: 15: 14: 14: 14) sts at beg of next row. 31 (31: 32: 34: 35: 37) sts.
Next row (RS): K to last 6 sts, K3tog tbl, K3.
Working all neck decreases as set by last row, dec 2 sts at neck edge of 2nd and foll 2 alt rows, then on 1 (1: 1: 2: 2: 2) foll 4th rows, then on foll 6th row. 19 (19: 20: 20: 21: 23) sts.
Work 3 rows, ending with a WS row.

Shape shoulder
Cast off 6 (6: 7: 7: 7: 8) sts at beg of next and foll alt row.
Work 1 row.
Cast off rem 7 (7: 6: 6: 7: 7) sts.
Mark positions for 6 buttons along left front opening edge – first button to come level with first RS row above hem border, last button to come 2.5 cm below neck shaping, and rem 4 buttons evenly spaced between.

RIGHT FRONT
Hem border
Cast on 29 (29: 29: 31: 31: 31) sts using 3¼mm (US 3) needles.
Work in g st for 4 rows, ending with a WS row.
Now work in border patt as given for back until this border measures approx 20 (21.5: 22.5: 24: 25: 27) cm, ending after patt row 9 and with a **RS** row.
Cast off knitwise (on **WS**).

Main section
With RS facing and using 3¼mm (US 3) needles, pick up and knit 48 (51: 54: 57: 60: 65) sts evenly along shorter row-end edge of hem border.
Now work in g st throughout as folls:
Work 1 row, ending with a WS row.
Next row (buttonhole row) (RS): K3, K2tog tbl, yfwd (to make a buttonhole), K to end.
Making a further 5 buttonholes in this way to correspond with positions marked for buttons along left front opening edge and noting that no further reference will be made to buttonholes, cont as folls:
Work 9 rows, ending with a WS row.
Working all side seam increases as set by back, inc 1 st at end of next and foll 10th row, then on 5 foll 12th rows. 55 (58: 61: 64: 67: 72) sts.
Complete to match left front, reversing shapings and working first 2 rows of neck shaping as folls:

Shape front neck
Next row (WS): K to last 14 (15: 15: 14: 14: 14) sts, cast off rem 14 (15: 15: 14: 14: 14) sts. 31 (31: 32: 34: 35: 37) sts.
Break yarn.
Rejoin yarn with RS facing and cont as folls:
Next row (RS): K3, K3tog, K to end.

SLEEVES (both alike)
Cast on 49 (51: 53: 55: 59: 61) sts using 3mm (US 2/3) needles.
Now work in g st throughout as folls:
Work 10 rows, ending with a WS row.
Change to 3¼mm (US 3) needles.
Work 4 rows, ending with a WS row.
Next row (RS): K3, M1, K to last 3 sts, M1, K3.
Working all sleeve increases as set by last row, inc 1 st at each end of 14th (14th: 14th: 16th: 16th: 16th) and every foll 14th (14th: 14th: 16th: 16th: 16th) row to 65 (63: 61: 79: 79: 77) sts, then on every foll 16th (16th: 16th: -: 18th: 18th) row until there are 73 (75: 77: -: 83: 85) sts.
Cont straight until sleeve measures 45 (46: 47: 48: 49: 50) cm, ending with a WS row.

Shape top
Cast off 4 (4: 5: 5: 6: 6) sts at beg of next 2 rows. 65 (67: 67: 69: 71: 73) sts.
Dec 1 st at each end of next 3 rows, then on foll alt row, then on foll 4th row, then on 3 foll 6th rows. 49 (51: 51: 53: 55: 57) sts.
Work 3 rows.
Dec 1 st at each end of next and foll 4th row, then on every foll alt row until 33 sts rem, then on foll 7 rows, ending with a WS row.
Cast off rem 19 sts.

MAKING UP
Press all pieces with a warm iron over a damp cloth.
Join both shoulder seams using back stitch or mattress stitch if preferred.
Join side seams. Join sleeve seams.
Insert sleeves into armholes.
Sew on buttons.

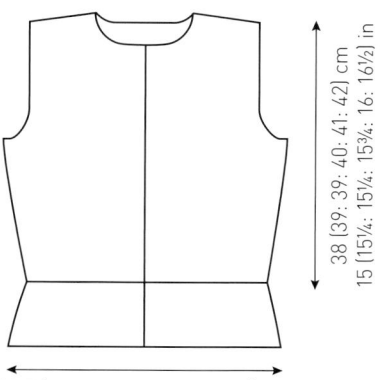

39.5 (42: 44.5: 47: 49.5: 53.5) cm
15½ (16½: 17½: 18½: 19½: 21) in

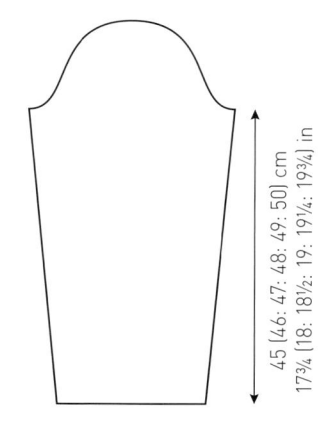

38 (39: 39: 40: 41: 42) cm
15 (15¼: 15¼: 15¾: 16: 16½) in

45 (46: 47: 48: 49: 50) cm
17¾ (18: 18½: 19: 19¼: 19¾) in

TYNE
Fitted guernsey style sweater

Recommendation
Suitable for the knitter with a little experience
Please see pages 42 - 45 for photographs.

	XS	S	M	L	XL	XXL	
To fit bust	**81**	**86**	**91**	**97**	**102**	**109**	cm
	32	34	36	38	40	43	in

Rowan Wool Cotton
| | 10 | 11 | 11 | 12 | 12 | 13 x 50gm |

Photographed in Antique

Needles
1 pair 3mm (no 11) (US 2/3) needles
1 pair 3¾mm (no 9) (US 5) needles
Cable needle

Tension
23 sts and 32 rows to 10 cm measured over stocking stitch using 3¾mm (US 5) needles.

Special abbreviations
C6B = slip next 3 sts onto cn and leave at back of work, K3, then K3 from cn; **C6F** = slip next 3 sts onto cn and leave at front of work, K3, then K3 from cn; **cn** = cable needle.

BACK and FRONT (both alike)
Cast on 128 (138: 143: 153: 158: 168) sts using 3mm (US 2/3) needles.
Row 1 (RS): K3, *P2, K3, rep from * to end.
Row 2: K5, *P3, K2, rep from * to last 3 sts, K3.
These 2 rows set the sts – 3 sts in g st at each end of row with sts between in rib.
Cont as set for a further 21 rows, ending with a **RS** row.
Change to 3¾mm (US 5) needles.
Row 24 (WS): Patt 8 (3: 8: 3: 8: 8) sts, K2tog, *P3, K2tog, rep from * to last 8 (3: 8: 3: 8: 8) sts, patt 8 (3: 8: 3: 8: 8) sts.
105 (111: 117: 123: 129: 137) sts.
Beg with a K row, work in st st for 2 rows, ending with a WS row.
Now work border as folls:
Row 1 (RS): K2 (5: 8: 1: 4: 8), P1, *K9, P1, rep from * to last 2 (5: 8: 1: 4: 8) sts, K2 (5: 8: 1: 4: 8).
Row 2: P1 (4: 7: 0: 3: 7), *K1, P1, K1, P7, rep from * to last 4 (7: 0: 3: 6: 0) sts, (K1, P1, K1) 1 (1: 0: 1: 1: 0) times, P1 (4: 0: 0: 3: 0).
Row 3: K0 (0: 0: 3: 0: 0), P0 (0: 1: 1: 0: 1), K0 (3: 5: 5: 2: 5), *P1, K3, P1, K5, rep from * to last 5 (8: 1: 4: 7: 1) sts, P1, K3 (3: 0: 3: 3: 0), P1 (1: 0: 0: 1: 0), K0 (3: 0: 0: 2: 0).
Row 4: P5 (0: 1: 4: 0: 1), K1 (0: 1: 1: 0: 1), P3 (2: 3: 3: 1: 3), *K1, P5, K1, P3, rep from * to last 6 (9: 2: 5: 8: 2) sts, K1, P5 (5: 1: 4: 5: 1), K0 (1: 0: 1: 0: 1), P0 (2: 0: 0: 1: 0).
Row 5: K6 (0: 2: 5: 0: 2), P1 (0: 1: 1: 0: 1), K1 (1: 1: 1: 0: 1), *P1, K7, P1, K1, rep from * to last 7 (0: 3: 6: 9: 3) sts, P1 (0: 1: 1: 1: 1), K6 (0: 2: 5: 7: 2), P0 (0: 0: 0: 1: 0).
Row 6: P7 (0: 3: 6: 9: 3), *K1, P9, rep from * to last 8 (1: 4: 7: 0: 4) sts, K1 (1: 1: 1: 0: 1), P7 (0: 3: 6: 0: 3).
Row 7: As row 5.
Row 8: As row 4.
Row 9: As row 3.
Row 10: As row 2.
Row 11: As row 1.
These 11 rows complete border.
Beg with a P row, cont in st st as folls:
Work 3 (3: 5: 5: 5: 5) rows, ending with a WS row.
Next row (RS): K9, K2tog tbl, K to last 11 sts, K2tog, K9.
Working all side seam decreases as set by last row, dec 1 st at each end of 6th and 2 foll 6th rows, then on 6 foll 4th rows.
85 (91: 97: 103: 109: 117) sts.
Work 13 (13: 15: 15: 15: 15) rows, ending with a WS row.
Inc 1 st at each end of next and 2 foll 6th rows.
91 (97: 103: 109: 115: 123) sts.
Work 3 rows, ending with a WS row.
Now work border for yoke as folls:
Row 1 (RS): K0 (3: 6: 9: 2: 6), *P1, K9, rep from * to last 1 (4: 7: 0: 3: 7) sts, P1 (1: 1: 0: 1: 1), K0 (3: 6: 0: 2: 6).
Row 2: P0 (2: 5: 0: 1: 5), K0 (1: 1: 0: 1: 1), P1 (1: 1: 0: 1: 1), *K1, P7, K1, P1, rep from * to last 0 (3: 6: 9: 2: 6) sts, K0 (1: 1: 1: 1: 1), P0 (2: 5: 7: 1: 5), K0 (0: 0: 1: 0: 0).
Row 3: Inc in first st, K0 (0: 3: 0: 0: 3), P0 (1: 1: 0: 1: 1), K1 (3: 3: 0: 3: 3), *P1, K5, P1, K3, rep from * to last 9 (2: 5: 8: 1: 5) sts, P1 (1: 1: 0: 1), K5 (0: 3: 5: 0: 3), P1 (0: 0: 1: 0: 0), K1 (0: 0: 0: 0: 0), inc in last st. 93 (99: 105: 111: 117: 125) sts.
Row 4: P0 (1: 0: 0: 0: 0), K0 (1: 0: 0: 1: 0), P4 (5: 0: 3: 5: 0), *K1, P3, K1, P5, rep from * to last 9 (2: 5: 8: 1: 5) sts, K1, P3 (1: 3: 3: 0: 3), K1 (0: 1: 1: 0: 1), P4 (0: 0: 3: 0: 0).
Row 5: P0 (1: 0: 0: 0: 0), K5 (7: 1: 4: 7: 1), *P1, K1, P1, K7, rep from * to last 8 (1: 4: 7: 0: 4) sts, P1 (1: 1: 1: 0: 1), K1 (0: 1: 1: 0: 1), P1 (0: 1: 1: 0: 1), K5 (0: 1: 4: 0: 1).
Row 6: P6 (9: 2: 5: 8: 2), *K1, P9, rep from * to last 7 (0: 3: 6: 9: 3) sts, K1 (0: 1: 1: 1: 1), P6 (0: 2: 5: 8: 2).
Row 7: Knit.
Row 8: Purl.
Row 9: Inc in first st, P to last st, inc in last st.
95 (101: 107: 113: 119: 127) sts.
Rows 10 and 11: Purl.
Row 12: P26 (29: 32: 35: 38: 42), M1P, P2, M1P, P39, M1P, P2, M1P, P26 (29: 32: 35: 38: 42). 99 (105: 111: 117: 123: 131) sts.
These 12 rows complete border for yoke.
Beg and ending rows as indicated and repeating the 14 and 16 row patt repeats throughout, now work in patt from chart for yoke as folls:
Inc 1 st at each end of 3rd and foll 6th row.
103 (109: 115: 121: 127: 135) sts.
Work 9 rows, ending with a WS row.

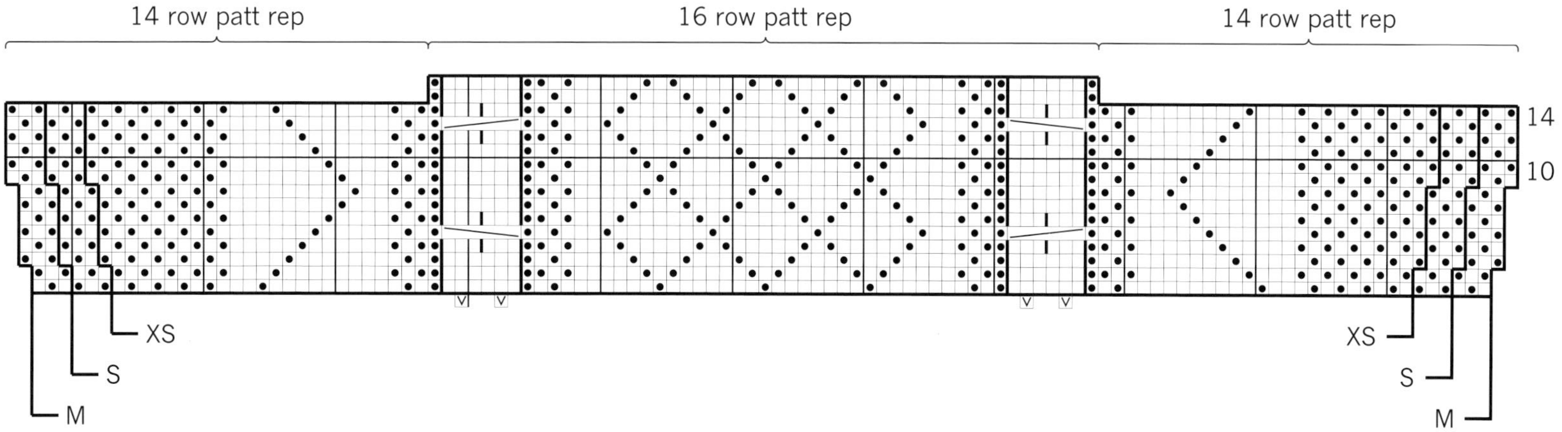

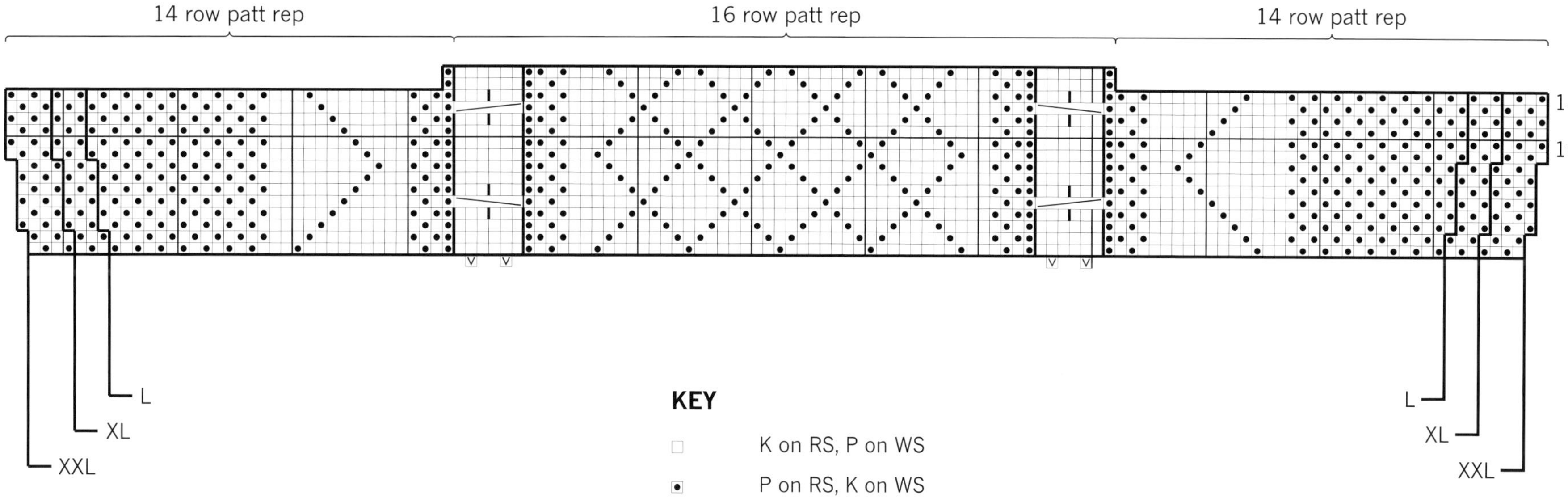

KEY

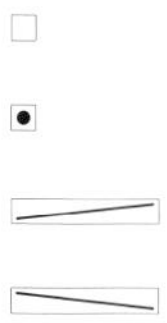

K on RS, P on WS

P on RS, K on WS

C6B

C6F

Shape armholes
Keeping patt correct, cast off 3 (3: 4: 4: 5: 5) sts at beg of next 2 rows.
97 (103: 107: 113: 117: 125) sts.
Dec 1 st at each end of next 1 (1: 1: 3: 3: 3) rows, then on foll 1 (2: 3: 3: 4: 6) alt rows, then on 0 (1: 1: 1: 1: 1) foll 4th row.
93 (95: 97: 99: 101: 105) sts.
Cont straight until armhole measures 15 (16: 16: 17: 18: 19) cm, ending with a **RS** row.
Change to 3mm (US 2/3) needles.
Next row (WS): P21 (22: 23: 24: 25: 27), K1, P6, K1, P35, K1, P6, K1, P21 (22: 23: 24: 25: 27).
Next row: K1 (2: 3: 0: 1: 3), (inc purlwise in next st, K3) 5 (5: 5: 6: 6: 6) times, *inc purlwise in next st, patt 6 sts, inc purlwise in next st*, (K3, inc purlwise in next st) 8 times, K3, rep from * to * once more, (K3, inc purlwise in next st) 5 (5: 5: 6: 6: 6) times, K1 (2: 3: 0: 1: 3).
115 (117: 119: 123: 125: 129) sts.
Next row: P1 (2: 3: 0: 1: 3), (K2, P3) 5 (5: 5: 6: 6: 6) times, *K2, patt 6 sts, K2*, (P3, K2) 8 times, P3, rep from * to * once more, (P3, K2) 5 (5: 5: 6: 6: 6) times, P1 (2: 3: 0: 1: 3).
Next row: K1 (2: 3: 0: 1: 3), (P2, K3) 5 (5: 5: 6: 6: 6) times, *P2, patt 6 sts, P2*, (K3, P2) 8 times, K3, rep from * to * once more, (K3, P2) 5 (5: 5: 6: 6: 6) times, K1 (2: 3: 0: 1: 3).
Rep last 2 rows until armhole measures 21 (22: 22: 23: 24: 25) cm, ending with a RS row.
Next row (WS): P1 (2: 3: 0: 1: 3), (K2tog, P3) 5 (5: 5: 6: 6: 6) times, *K2tog, patt 6 sts, K2tog *, (P3, K2tog) 8 times, P3, rep from * to * once more, (P3, K2tog) 5 (5: 5: 6: 6: 6) times, P1 (2: 3: 0: 1: 3).
Cast off rem 93 (95: 97: 99: 101: 105) sts in patt.

SLEEVES (both alike)
Cast on 62 (64: 66: 68: 72: 74) sts using 3mm (US 2/3) needles.
Row 1 (RS): K0 (1: 2: 3: 0: 1), P2, *K3, P2, rep from * to last 0 (1: 2: 3: 0: 1) sts, K0 (1: 2: 3: 0: 1).
Row 2: P0 (1: 2: 3: 0: 1), K2, *P3, K2, rep from * to last 0 (1: 2: 3: 0: 1) sts, P0 (1: 2: 3: 0: 1).
These 2 rows form rib.
Work in rib for a further 21 rows, inc 1 st at each end of 13th row and ending with a **RS** row. 64 (66: 68: 70: 74: 76) sts.
Change to 3¾mm (US 5) needles.
Row 24 (WS): P1 (2: 3: 4: 1: 2), K2tog, *P3, K2tog, rep from * to last 1 (2: 3: 4: 1: 2) sts, P1 (2: 3: 4: 1: 2). 51 (53: 55: 57: 59: 61) sts.

Beg with a K row, work in st st for 2 rows, ending with a WS row.
Now work border as folls:
Row 1 (RS): Inc in first st, K4 (5: 6: 7: 8: 9), P1, *K9, P1, rep from * to last 5 (6: 7: 8: 9: 10) sts, K4 (5: 6: 7: 8: 9), inc in last st.
53 (55: 57: 59: 61: 63) sts.
Row 2: P0 (0: 0: 0: 1: 0), K0 (0: 0: 1: 1: 0), P5 (6: 7: 7: 7: 0), *K1, P1, K1, P7, rep from * to last 8 (9: 0: 1: 2: 3) sts, K1 (1: 0: 1: 1: 1), P1 (1: 0: 0: 1: 1), K1 (1: 0: 0: 0: 1), P5 (6: 0: 0: 0: 0).
Row 3: K0 (0: 0: 1: 2: 3), P0 (0: 1: 1: 1: 1), K4 (5: 5: 5: 5: 5), *P1, K3, P1, K5, rep from * to last 9 (0: 1: 2: 3: 4) sts, P1 (0: 1: 1: 1: 1), K3 (0: 0: 1: 2: 3), P1 (0: 0: 0: 0: 0), K4 (0: 0: 0: 0: 0).
Row 4: P0 (0: 1: 2: 3: 4), K0 (1: 1: 1: 1: 1), P3, *K1, P5, K1, P3, rep from * to last 0 (1: 2: 3: 4: 5) sts, K0 (1: 1: 1: 1: 1), P0 (0: 1: 2: 3: 4).
Row 5: K0 (1: 2: 3: 4: 5), P1, K1, *P1, K7, P1, K1, rep from * to last 1 (2: 3: 4: 5: 6) sts, P1, K0 (1: 2: 3: 4: 5).
Row 6: P1 (2: 3: 4: 5: 6), *K1, P9, rep from * to last 2 (3: 4: 5: 6: 7) sts, K1, P1 (2: 3: 4: 5: 6).
Row 7: K6 (7: 8: 0: 0: 1), P1 (1: 1: 0: 1: 1), *K9, P1, rep from * to last 6 (7: 8: 9: 0: 1) sts, K6 (7: 8: 9: 0: 1).
Rows 8 to 10: As rows 2 to 4.
Row 11: Inc in first st, K0 (0: 1: 2: 3: 4), P0 (1: 1: 1: 1: 1), K1, *P1, K7, P1, K1, rep from * to last 1 (2: 3: 4: 5: 6) sts, P0 (1: 1: 1: 1: 1), K0 (0: 1: 2: 3: 4), inc in last st.
55 (57: 59: 61: 63: 65) sts.
Row 12: P2 (3: 4: 5: 6: 7), *K1, P9, rep from * to last 3 (4: 5: 6: 7: 8) sts, K1, P2 (3: 4: 5: 6: 7).
These 12 rows complete border.
Beg with a K row, cont in st st as folls:
Work 8 rows, ending with a WS row.
Next row (RS): K3, M1, K to last 3 sts, M1, K3.
Working all sleeve increases as set by last row, inc 1 st at each end of 10th and every foll 10th row to 71 (69: 69: 67: 79: 77) sts, then on every foll 12th row until there are 73 (75: 77: 79: 83: 85) sts.
Cont straight until sleeve measures 46 (47: 48: 49: 50: 51) cm, ending with a WS row.
Shape top
Cast off 3 (3: 4: 4: 5: 5) sts at beg of next 2 rows.
67 (69: 69: 71: 73: 75) sts.
Dec 1 st at each end of next 7 rows, then on every foll alt row until 25 sts rem, then on foll 3 rows, ending with a WS row.
Cast off rem 19 sts.

MAKING UP
Press all pieces with a warm iron over a damp cloth.
Join both shoulder seams using back stitch or mattress stitch if preferred, leaving 39 (40: 40: 41: 41: 41) cm open at centre of seam for neck opening. Join side seams, leaving seams open for first 24 rows. Join sleeve seams. Insert sleeves into armholes.

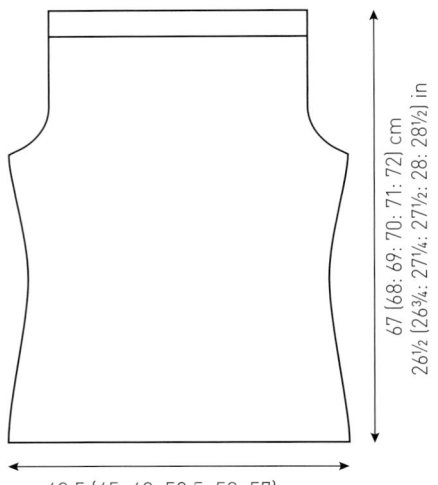

67 (68: 69: 70: 71: 72) cm
26½ (26¾: 27¼: 27½: 28: 28½) in

43.5 (45: 48: 50.5: 53: 57) cm
17 (18: 19: 20: 21: 22½) in

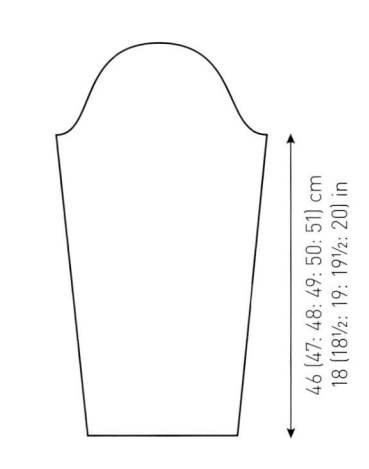

46 (47: 48: 49: 50: 51) cm
18 (18½: 19: 19½: 20) in

RIPLEY
Oversized tartan sweater

Recommendation
Suitable for the more experience knitter
Please see pages 54 - 57 for photographs.

	XS	S	M	L	XL	XXL	
To fit bust	81	86	91	97	102	109	cm
	32	34	36	38	40	43	in

Rowan Cocoon and Kid Classic
A Cocoon Scree
    6   6   7   7   8   8x 100gm
B Cocoon Moon
        3   3   3   4   4   4x 100gm
C Cocoon Shale
        1   1   2   2   2   2x 100gm
D Cocoon Alpine
        1   1   1   1   1   1x 100gm
E Kid Classic Nightly
        2   2   2   2   2   2 x 50gm

Needles
1 pair 5mm (no 6) (US 8) needles
1 pair 6mm (no 4) (US 10) needles

Tension
16 sts and 20 rows to 10 cm measured over patterned stocking stitch using 6mm (US 10) needles.

Pattern note: Yarn E (Kid Classic) is used **DOUBLE** throughout.

BACK
Cast on 118 (124: 128: 134: 138: 146) sts using 5mm (US 8) needles and yarn A.
Row 1 (RS): K3 (1: 3: 1: 3: 2), *P2, K3, rep from * to last 0 (3: 0: 3: 0: 4) sts, P0 (2: 0: 2: 0: 2), K0 (1: 0: 1: 0: 2).
Row 2: P3 (1: 3: 1: 3: 2), *K2, P3, rep from * to last 0 (3: 0: 3: 0: 4) sts, K0 (2: 0: 2: 0: 2), P0 (1: 0: 1: 0: 2).
These 2 rows form rib.
Work in rib for a further 7 rows, ending with a **RS** row.
Change to 6mm (US 10) needles.
Row 10 (WS): P3 (1: 3: 1: 3: 2), *K2tog, P3, rep from * to last 0 (3: 0: 3: 0: 4) sts, (K2tog) 0 (1: 0: 1: 0: 1) times, P0 (1: 0: 1: 0: 2).
95 (99: 103: 107: 111: 117) sts.
Beg and ending rows as indicated, using the **intarsia** technique as described on the information page and repeating the 34 row patt repeat throughout (and remembering yarn E is used **DOUBLE**), cont in patt from chart, which is worked entirely in st st beg with a K row, as folls:
Cont in patt until back measures 44 (44: 45: 45: 45: 45) cm, ending with a WS row.
Shape armholes
Keeping patt correct, cast off 5 sts at beg of next 2 rows. 85 (89: 93: 97: 101: 107) sts.
Cont straight until armhole measures 24 (25: 25: 26: 27: 28) cm, ending with a WS row.
Shape shoulders and back neck
Cast off 6 (7: 7: 7: 8: 9) sts at beg of next 2 rows, then 7 (7: 7: 8: 8: 9) sts at beg of foll 2 rows. 59 (61: 65: 67: 69: 71) sts.
Next row (RS): Cast off 7 (7: 8: 8: 8: 9) sts, patt until there are 11 (11: 12: 12: 13: 13) sts on right needle and turn, leaving rem sts on a holder.
Work each side of neck separately.
Cast off 4 sts at beg of next row.
Cast off rem 7 (7: 8: 8: 9: 9) sts.
With RS facing, rejoin yarns to rem sts, cast off centre 23 (25: 25: 27: 27: 27) sts, patt to end.
Complete to match first side, reversing shapings.

FRONT
Work as given for back until 8 (8: 8: 10: 10: 10) rows less have been worked than on back to start of shoulder shaping, ending with a WS row.

Shape front neck
Next row (RS): Patt 34 (35: 37: 39: 41: 44) sts and turn, leaving rem sts on a holder.
Work each side of neck separately.
Keeping patt correct, dec 1 st at neck edge of next 4 rows, then on foll 1 (1: 1: 2: 2: 2) alt rows. 29 (30: 32: 33: 35: 38) sts.
Work 1 row, ending with a WS row.
Shape shoulder
Cast off 6 (7: 7: 7: 8: 9) sts at beg of next and foll 0 (2: 1: 0: 2: 2) alt rows, then 7 (-: 8: 8: -: -) sts at beg of foll 2 (-: 1: 2: -: -) alt rows **and at same time** dec 1 st at neck edge of next and foll alt row.
Work 1 row.
Cast off rem 7 (7: 8: 8: 9: 9) sts.
With RS facing, rejoin yarns to rem sts, cast off centre 17 (19: 19: 19: 19: 19) sts, patt to end.
Complete to match first side, reversing shapings.

SLEEVES (both alike)
Cast on 48 (52: 52: 54: 56: 56) sts using 5mm (US 8) needles and yarn A.
Row 1 (RS): K3 (0: 0: 1: 2: 2), *P2, K3, rep from * to last 0 (2: 2: 3: 4: 4) sts, P0 (2: 2: 2: 2: 2), K0 (0: 0: 1: 2: 2).
Row 2: P3 (0: 0: 1: 2: 2), *K2, P3, rep from * to last 0 (2: 2: 3: 4: 4) sts, K0 (2: 2: 2: 2: 2), P0 (0: 0: 1: 2: 2).
These 2 rows form rib.
Work in rib for a further 7 rows, ending with a **RS** row.
Change to 6mm (US 10) needles.
Row 10 (WS): P3 (0: 0: 1: 2: 2), *K2tog, P3, rep from * to last 0 (2: 2: 3: 4: 4) sts, (K2tog) 0 (1: 1: 1: 1: 1) times, P0 (0: 0: 1: 2: 2).
39 (41: 41: 43: 45: 45) sts.
Beg and ending rows as indicated (and remembering yarn E is used **DOUBLE**), cont in patt from chart as folls:
Inc 1 st at each end of 3rd and 0 (0: 0: 0: 0: 1) foll alt row, then on every foll 4th row until there are 75 (81: 81: 81: 87: 89) sts, then on 1 (0: 0: 1: 0: 0) foll 6th row, taking inc sts into patt.
77 (81: 81: 83: 87: 89) sts.
Cont straight until sleeve measures 48 (49: 49: 50: 51: 52) cm, ending with a WS row.
Cast off.

KEY
- A (empty square)
- B (×)
- C (·)
- D (○)
- E (■)

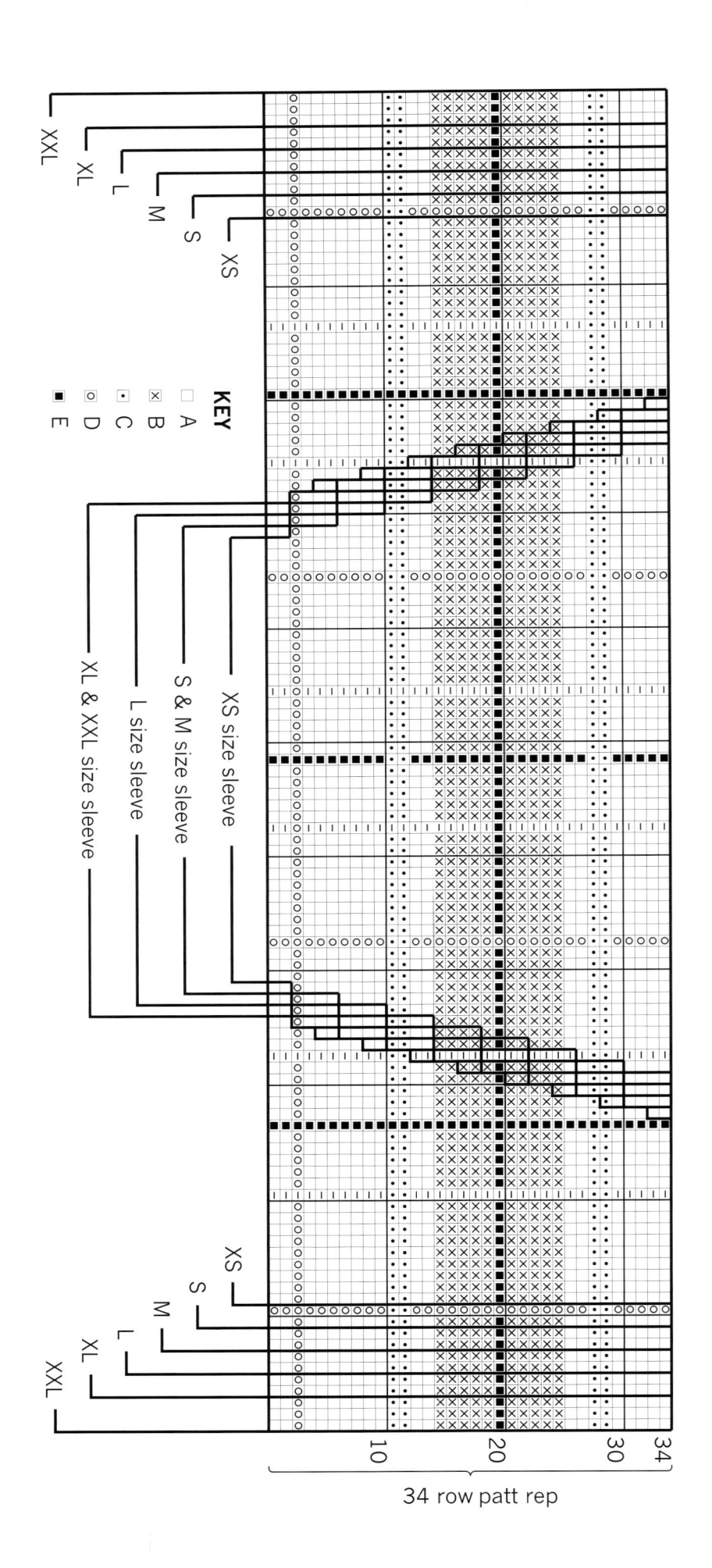

34 row patt rep

Continued on next page...

ALANNA
Snug openwork scarf

Recommendation
Suitable for the knitter with a little experience
Please see pages 52 & 53 for photographs.

Rowan Cocoon
5 x 100gm
Photographed in Moon

Needles
1 pair 8mm (no 0) (US 11) needles

Tension
14 sts and 15 rows to 10 cm measured over pattern using 8mm (US 11) needles.

Finished size
Completed scarf is 35 cm (14 in) wide and 200 cm (78½ in) long.

SCARF
Cast on 49 sts using 8mm (US 11) needles. Work in patt as folls:
Row 1 (WS): Knit.
Row 2: Knit.
Row 3: K3, P1, *(yrn) twice, keeping yarn at front (WS) of work slip next 2 sts, P3tog, pass 2 slipped sts over, (yrn) twice, P1, rep from * to last 3 sts, K3.
Row 4: K4, *(K1, P1) into double yrn of previous row, K1, (P1, K1) into double yrn of previous row, K1, rep from * to last 3 sts, K3.
Rows 5 and 6: Knit.
Row 7: K3, P3tog, *(yrn) twice, P1, (yrn) twice, keeping yarn at front (WS) of work slip next 2 sts, P3tog, pass 2 slipped sts over, rep from * to last 7 sts, (yrn) twice, P1, (yrn) twice, P3tog, K3.
Row 8: K4, *(P1, K1) into double yrn of previous row, K1, (K1, P1) into double yrn of previous row, K1, rep from * to last 3 sts, K3.
These 8 rows form patt.
Cont in patt until scarf measures approx 200 cm, ending after patt row 2 or 6 and with a WS row.
Cast off.

RIPLEY – Continued from previous page.

MAKING UP
Press all pieces with a warm iron over a damp cloth.
Join right shoulder seam using back stitch or mattress stitch if preferred.

Neckband
With RS facing, using 5mm (US 8) needles and yarn A, pick up and knit 14 (14: 14: 15: 15: 15) sts down left side of neck, 17 (19: 19: 19: 19: 19) sts from front, 14 (14: 14: 15: 15: 15) sts up right side of neck, then 32 (34: 34: 36: 36: 36) sts from back. 77 (81: 81: 85: 85: 85) sts.
Row 1 (WS): P2, *inc in next st, P3, rep from * to last 3 sts, inc in next st, P2.
96 (101: 101: 106: 106: 106) sts.
Row 2: K2, *P2, K3, rep from * to last 4 sts, P2, K2.
Row 3: P2, *K2, P3, rep from * to last 4 sts, K2, P2.
Last 2 rows form rib.
Work in rib for a further 3 rows, ending with a **RS** row.
Row 7 (WS): P2, *K2tog, P3, rep from * to last 4 sts, K2tog, P2. 77 (81: 81: 85: 85: 85) sts.
Cast off in rib.

Join left shoulder and neckband seam. Mark points along row-end edges of sleeves 3 cm down from cast-off edges. Matching these marked points to top of side seams, sleeve cast-off edges to armhole row-end edges, and centre of sleeve cast-off edges to shoulder seams, sew sleeves into armholes. Join side and sleeve seams.

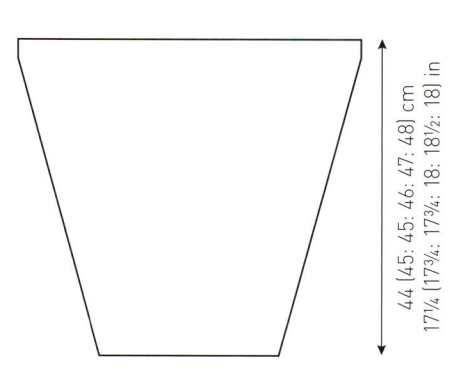

44 (45: 45: 46: 47: 48) cm
17¼ (17¾: 17¾: 18: 18½: 18) in

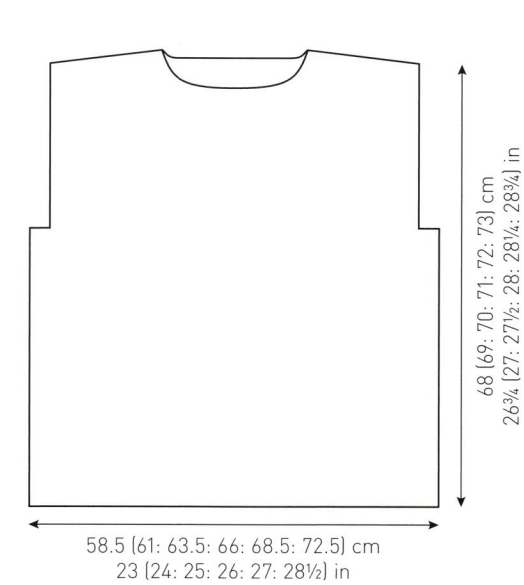

58.5 (61: 63.5: 66: 68.5: 72.5) cm
23 (24: 25: 26: 27: 28½) in

68 (69: 70: 71: 72: 73) cm
26¾ (27: 27½: 28: 28¼: 28¾) in

BRYN
Understated polo neck sweater

Recommendation
Suitable for the knitter with a little experience
Please see pages 48-51 for photographs.

	XS	S	M	L	XL	XXL	
To fit bust	81	86	91	97	102	109	cm
	32	34	36	38	40	43	in

Rowan Baby Alpaca DK
11 11 12 12 13 14 x 50gm
Photographed in Southdown

Needles
1 pair 3mm (no 11) (US 2/3) needles
1 pair 3¾mm (no 9) (US 5) needles

Tension
23 sts and 31 rows to 10 cm measured over stocking stitch using 3¾mm (US 5) needles.

BACK
Hem border
Cast on 26 (26: 26: 28: 28: 28) sts using 3mm (US 2/3) needles.
Rows 1 to 3: Knit.
Row 4 (WS): K2, *yrn, P2tog, rep from * to last 2 sts, K2.
Rows 5 to 9: Knit.
Row 10: K2, P to last 2 sts, K2.
Rows 11 and 12: Knit.
These 12 rows form border patt.
Cont in patt until hem border measures approx 45.5 (48: 50.5: 53: 55.5: 59.5) cm, ending after patt row 2 and with a WS row.
Cast off.

Main section
With RS facing and using 3¾mm (US 5) needles, beg at cast-on edge, pick up and knit 105 (111: 117: 123: 129: 137) sts evenly along one row-end edge of hem border.
Beg with a P row, now work in st st throughout as folls:
Cont straight until back measures 34 (34: 35: 35: 35: 35) cm **from lower edge of hem border**, ending with a WS row.

Shape armholes
Cast off 5 (5: 6: 6: 7: 7) sts at beg of next 2 rows. 95 (101: 105: 111: 115: 123) sts.
Dec 1 st at each end of next 5 (7: 7: 9: 9: 11) rows, then on foll 2 (2: 3: 3: 4: 4) alt rows, then on foll 4th row. 79 (81: 83: 85: 87: 91) sts.
Cont straight until armhole measures 19 (20: 20: 21: 22: 23) cm, ending with a WS row.

Shape shoulders and back neck
Cast off 6 (6: 6: 6: 6: 7) sts at beg of next 2 rows. 67 (69: 71: 73: 75: 77) sts.
Next row (RS): Cast off 6 (6: 6: 6: 6: 7) sts, K until there are 9 (9: 10: 10: 11: 11) sts on right needle and turn, leaving rem sts on a holder.
Work each side of neck separately.
Cast off 4 sts at beg of next row.
Cast off rem 5 (5: 6: 6: 7: 7) sts.
With RS facing, rejoin yarn to rem sts, cast off centre 37 (39: 39: 41: 41: 41) sts, K to end.
Complete to match first side, reversing shapings.

FRONT
Work as given for back until 8 (8: 8: 10: 10: 10) rows less have been worked than on back to start of shoulder shaping, ending with a WS row.

Shape front neck
Next row (RS): K23 (23: 24: 25: 26: 28) and turn, leaving rem sts on a holder.
Work each side of neck separately.
Dec 1 st at neck edge of next 4 rows, then on foll 1 (1: 1: 2: 2: 2) alt rows.
18 (18: 19: 19: 20: 22) sts.
Work 1 row, ending with a WS row.

Shape shoulder
Cast off 6 (6: 6: 6: 6: 7) sts at beg of next and foll alt rows **and at same time** dec 1 st at neck edge of next row.
Work 1 row.
Cast off rem 5 (5: 6: 6: 7: 7) sts.
With RS facing, rejoin yarn to rem sts, cast off centre 33 (35: 35: 35: 35: 35) sts, K to end.
Complete to match first side, reversing shapings.

SLEEVES (both alike)
Cuff border
Cast on 26 (26: 26: 28: 28: 28) sts using 3mm (US 2/3) needles.
Work in border patt as given for hem border of back until this border measures approx 24 (25: 26: 27: 28: 29) cm, ending after patt row 2 and with a WS row.
Cast off.

Main section
With RS facing and using 3¾mm (US 5) needles, beg at cast-on edge, pick up and knit 56 (58: 60: 62: 64: 66) sts evenly along one row-end edge of cuff border.
Beg with a P row, now work in st st throughout as folls:
Work 3 rows, ending with a WS row.
Next row (RS): K3, M1, K to last 3 sts, M1, K3.
Working all sleeve increases as set by last row, inc 1 st at each end of 12th (14th: 14th: 14th: 12th: 12th) and every foll 12th (14th: 14th: 14th: 12th: 12th) row to 62 (74: 74: 76: 74: 74) sts, then on every foll 14th (-: 16th: 16th: 14th: 14th) row until there are 72 (-: 76: 78: 82: 84) sts.
Cont straight until sleeve measures 45 (46: 47: 48: 49: 50) cm, ending with a WS row.

Shape top
Cast off 5 (5: 6: 6: 7: 7) sts at beg of next 2 rows. 62 (64: 64: 66: 68: 70) sts.
Dec 1 st at each end of next 3 rows, then on foll alt row, then on 6 foll 4th rows.
42 (44: 44: 46: 48: 50) sts.

Continued on next page...

FOGGY
Long-line fairisle scarf

Recommendation
Suitable for the knitter with a little experience
Please see pages 33 for photographs.

Rowan Alpaca Cotton
A	Storm	3	x 50gm
B	Thunder	2	x 50gm
C	Raindrop	1	x 50gm

Needles
1 pair 5mm (no 6) (US 8) needles
1 pair 5½mm (no 5) (US 9) needles

Tension
16 sts and 22 rows to 10 cm measured over patterned stocking stitch using 5½mm (US 9) needles.

Finished size
Completed scarf is 18 cm (7 in) wide and 244 cm (96 in) long.

SCARF
Cast on 28 sts using 5mm (US 8) needles and yarn A.
Work in g st for 6 rows, ending with a WS row.
Change to 5½mm (US 9) needles.
Beg and ending rows as indicated, using a combination of the **intarsia** and **fairisle** techniques as described on the information page and repeating the 46 row patt repeat throughout, cont in patt from chart, which is worked mainly in st st beg with a K row, as folls:
Cont straight until scarf measures approx 242 cm, ending after chart row 22 or 46 and with a WS row.
Break off contrasts and cont using yarn A only.
Change to 5mm (US 8) needles.
Work in g st for 6 rows, ending with a WS row.
Cast off.

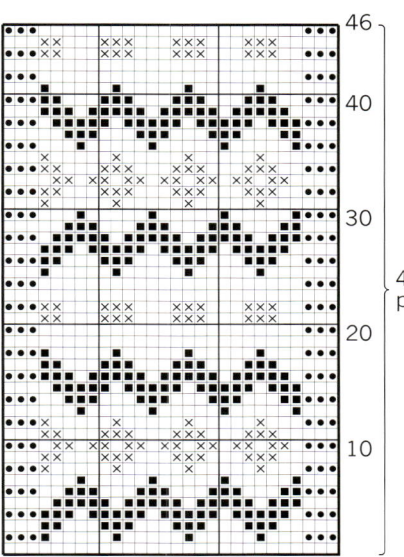

KEY
- A ☐ K on RS, P on WS
- A • P on RS, K on WS
- B ■ K on RS, P on WS
- C ☒ K on RS, P on WS

46 row patt rep

BRYN – Continued from previous page.

Work 1 row.
Dec 1 st at each end of next and every foll alt row until 38 sts rem, then on foll 7 rows, ending with a WS row.
Cast off rem 24 sts.

MAKING UP
Press all pieces with a warm iron over a damp cloth.
Join right shoulder seam using back stitch or mattress stitch if preferred.

Collar
With RS facing and using 3mm (US 2/3) needles, pick up and knit 12 (12: 12: 14: 14: 14) sts down left side of neck, 33 (35: 35: 35: 35: 35) sts from front, 12 (12: 12: 14: 14: 14) sts up right side of neck, then 48 (50: 50: 52: 52: 52) sts from back.
105 (109: 109: 115: 115: 115) sts.
Work in g st for 6 rows, ending with a **RS** row.

Now work in rib as folls:
Row 1 (WS): P1, *K1 tbl, P1, rep from * to end.
Row 2: K1 tbl, *P1, K1 tbl, rep from * to end.
These 2 rows form rib.
Work in rib for a further 4 rows, ending with a **RS** row.

Change to 3¾mm (US 5) needles.
Cont in rib until collar measures 13 cm **from top of g st section**.
Cast off in rib.
Join left shoulder and collar seam.
Join side seams. Join sleeve seams. Insert sleeves into armholes.

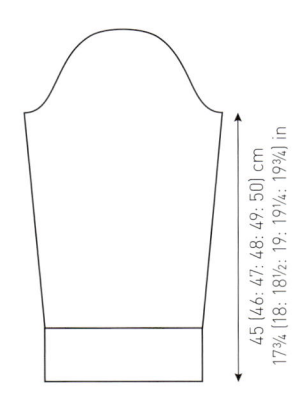

45 (46: 47: 48: 49: 50) cm
17¾ (18: 18½: 19: 19¼: 19¾) in

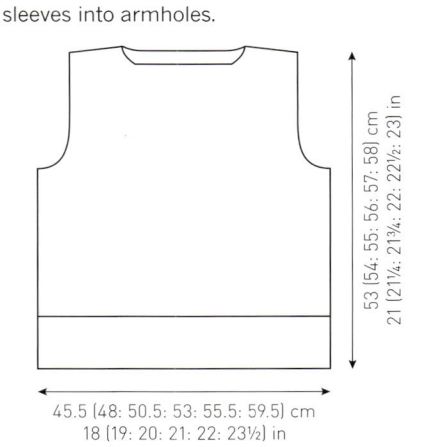

53 (54: 55: 56: 57: 58) cm
21 (21¼: 21¾: 22: 22½: 23) in

45.5 (48: 50.5: 53: 55.5: 59.5) cm
18 (19: 20: 21: 22: 23½) in

CARIS
Striped raglan sweater

Recommendation
Suitable for the knitter with a little experience
Please see pages 46 & 47 for photographs.

	XS	S	M	L	XL	XXL	
To fit bust	**81**	**86**	**91**	**97**	**102**	**109**	cm
	32	34	36	38	40	43	in

Rowan Kidsilk Haze and Fine Lace
A Kidsilk Haze Smoke
  3   3   4   4   5   5 x 25gm
B Fine Lace Gunmetal
  2   2   2   2   3   3 x 50gm
C Kidsilk Haze Pearl
  2   3   3   4   4   5 x 25gm
D Fine Lace Porcelain
  2   2   2   2   3   3 x 50gm

Needles
1 pair 3mm (no 11) (US 2/3) needles
1 pair 3¼mm (no 10) (US 3) needles

Tension
23 sts and 31 rows to 10 cm measured over stocking stitch using 3¼mm (US 3) needles and one strand each of Kidsilk Haze and Fine Lace held together.

Special note: We found it preferable to knit the two yarns together from separate balls rather than winding them together.

BACK
Cast on 94 (100: 106: 112: 118: 126) sts using 3mm (US 2/3) needles and one strand each of yarns A and B held together.
Beg with a K row, work in st st throughout as folls:
Work 8 rows, ending with a WS row.
Change to 3¼mm (US 3) needles.
Work 12 rows.
Join in one strand each of yarns C and D held together.
Using one strand each of yarns C and D held together, work 10 rows.
Next row (RS): Using one strand each of yarns A and B held together K3, K2tog, K to last 5 sts, K2tog tbl, K3.
Working all side seam decreases as set by last row, cont as folls:
Using one strand each of yarns A and B held together, work 9 rows, ending with a WS row.
Last 20 rows form striped st st and beg side seam shaping.
Cont in striped st st, dec 1 st at each end of next and 2 (2: 2: 3: 3: 3) foll 10th rows, then on 1 (1: 1: 0: 0: 0) foll 8th row.
84 (90: 96: 102: 108: 116) sts.
Work 21 rows, ending with a WS row.
Next row (RS): K3, M1, K to last 3 sts, M1, K3.
Working all side seam increases as set by last row, inc 1 st at each end of 10th and foll 10th row, then on 2 foll 12th rows.
94 (100: 106: 112: 118: 126) sts.
Work 13 rows, ending after 8 (8: 8: 10: 10: 10) rows using one strand each of yarns C and D held together and with a WS row.
Shape raglan armholes
Keeping stripes correct, cast off 4 (4: 4: 4: 5: 5) sts at beg of next 2 rows.
86 (92: 98: 104: 108: 116) sts.
Work 2 rows, ending with a WS row.
Next row (RS): K1, K2tog, K to last 3 sts, K2tog tbl, K1.
Working all raglan armhole decreases as set by last row, dec 1 st at each end of 4th (4th: 4th: 4th: 4th: 2nd) and 2 (2: 1: 0: 1: 0) foll 4th rows, then on foll 10 (12: 15: 18: 18: 22) alt rows.
58 (60: 62: 64: 66: 68) sts.
Work 1 row, ending with a WS row.
Cast off.

FRONT
Work as given for back until 72 (74: 76: 78: 80: 82) sts rem in raglan armhole shaping.
Work 1 row, ending with a WS row.
Shape front neck
Next row (RS): K1, K2tog, K9 and turn, leaving rem sts on a holder. 11 sts.
Work each side of neck separately.
Keeping stripes correct, dec 1 st at neck edge of next 4 rows, then on foll alt row **and at same time** dec 1 st at raglan armhole edge of 2nd and foll 2 alt rows. 3 sts.
Work 1 row, ending with a WS row.
Next row (RS): Sl 1, K2tog, psso.
Next row: P1 and fasten off.
With RS facing, rejoin appropriate yarns to rem sts, cast off centre 48 (50: 52: 54: 56: 58) sts, K to last 3 sts, K2tog tbl, K1. 11 sts.
Complete to match first side, reversing shapings.

LEFT SLEEVE
Cast on 44 (46: 48: 52: 54: 58) sts using 3mm (US 2/3) needles and one strand each of yarns C and D held together.
Beg with a K row, work in st st throughout as folls:
Work 8 rows, ending with a WS row.
Change to 3¼mm (US 3) needles.
Shape thumb opening
Next row (RS): K33 (34: 35: 37: 38: 40) and turn, leaving rem 11 (12: 13: 15: 16: 18) sts on a holder.
Work 12 rows on this set of 33 (34: 35: 37: 38: 40) sts, ending with a RS row.
Break yarn and leave sts on a second holder.
Return to 11 (12: 13: 15: 16: 18) sts on first holder, rejoin yarn with RS facing and K to end.
Work 12 rows on this set of 11 (12: 13: 15: 16: 18) sts, ending with a **RS** row.
Join sections
Next row (WS): P across 11 (12: 13: 15: 16: 18) sts on needle, then with WS facing P across 33 (34: 35: 37: 38: 40) sts of section on holder. 44 (46: 48: 52: 54: 58) sts.
Thumb opening is now complete.
**Working all sleeve increases in same way as back side seam increases, cont as folls:
Work 6 (8: 10: 14: 16: 20) rows, inc 0 (0: 0: 0: 1: 1) st at each end of 15th of these rows and ending with a WS row.
44 (46: 48: 52: 56: 60) sts.

Join in one strand each of yarns A and B held together.
Beg with 10 rows using one strand each of yarns A and B held together, now work in striped st st as given for back and cont as folls:
Inc 1 st at each end of 7th (5th: 3rd: next: 9th: 5th) and 12 (11: 10: 3: 7: 5) foll 10th rows, then on 0 (1: 2: 8: 4: 6) foll 12th rows.
70 (72: 74: 76: 80: 84) sts.
Work 11 (11: 11: 13: 13: 13) rows, ending after 8 (8: 8: 10: 10: 10) rows using one strand each of yarns C and D held together and with a WS row.

Shape raglan
Keeping stripes correct, cast off 4 (4: 4: 4: 5: 5) sts at beg of next 2 rows.
62 (64: 66: 68: 70: 74) sts.
Working all raglan decreases in same way as back raglan armhole decreases, dec 1 st at each end of next (3rd: 3rd: 3rd: 3rd: 3rd) and 0 (1: 1: 2: 3: 3) foll 4th rows, then on foll 15 (14: 15: 14: 14: 15) alt rows.
30 (32: 32: 34: 34: 36) sts.
Work 1 row, ending with a WS row.

Shape for neck
Dec 1 st at each end of next row, then cast off 9 (9: 9: 10: 10: 11) sts at beg of foll row.
19 (21: 21: 22: 22: 23) sts.
Dec 1 st at beg of next row, then cast off 9 (10: 10: 10: 10: 11) sts at beg of foll row.
Cast off rem 9 (10: 10: 11: 11: 11) sts.

RIGHT SLEEVE
Work as given for left sleeve to start of thumb opening.

Shape thumb opening
Next row (RS): K11 (12: 13: 15: 16: 18) and turn, leaving rem 33 (34: 35: 37: 38: 40) sts on a holder.
Work 12 rows on this set of 11 (12: 13: 15: 16: 18) sts, ending with a **RS** row.
Break yarn and leave sts on a second holder.
Return to 33 (34: 35: 37: 38: 40) sts on first holder, rejoin yarn with RS facing and K to end.
Work 12 rows on this set of 33 (34: 35: 37: 38: 40) sts, ending with a **RS** row.

Join sections
Next row (WS): P across 33 (34: 35: 37: 38: 40) sts on needle, then with WS facing P across 11 (12: 13: 15: 16: 18) sts of section on holder.
44 (46: 48: 52: 54: 58) sts.
Thumb opening is now complete.
Work as given for left sleeve from ** to start of neck shaping.

Shape for neck
Cast off 10 (10: 10: 11: 11: 12) sts at beg and dec 1 st at end of next row.
19 (21: 21: 22: 22: 23) sts.
Work 1 row.
Cast off 9 (10: 10: 10: 10: 11) sts at beg and dec 1 st at end of next row.
Work 1 row.
Cast off rem 9 (10: 10: 11: 11: 11) sts.

MAKING UP
Press all pieces with a warm iron over a damp cloth.
Join both front and right back raglan armhole seams using back stitch or mattress stitch if preferred.

Neckband
With RS facing, using 3¼mm (US 3) needles and one strand each of yarns C and D held together, pick up and knit 26 (28: 28: 30: 30: 32) sts from top of left sleeve, 8 sts down left side of neck, 48 (50: 52: 54: 56: 58) sts from front, 8 sts up right side of neck, 26 (28: 28: 30: 30: 32) sts from top of right sleeve, and
56 (58: 60: 62: 64: 66) sts from back.
172 (180: 184: 192: 196: 204) sts.
Beg with a P row, work in st st for 10 rows, ending with a **RS** row.
Change to 3mm (US 2/3) needles.
Work a further 7 rows, ending with a WS row.
Cast off, taking care not to cast off too tightly.
Join left back raglan and neckband seam.
Join side and sleeve seams.

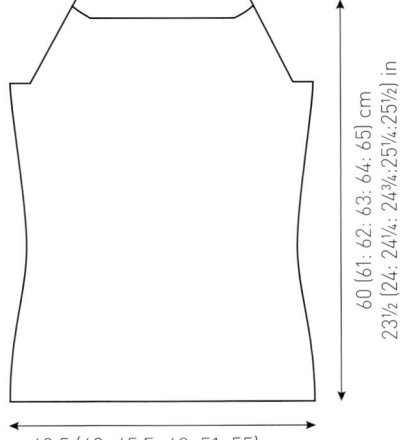

40.5 (43: 45.5: 48: 51: 55) cm
16 (17: 18: 19: 20: 21½) in

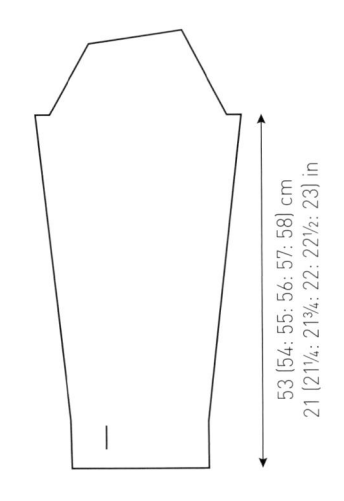

60 (61: 62: 63: 64: 65) cm
23½ (24: 24¼: 24¾: 25¼: 25½) in

53 (54: 55: 56: 57: 58) cm
21 (21¼: 21¾: 22: 22½: 23) in

INFORMATION
A guide to assist with techniques & finishing touches

TENSION
Achieving the correct tension has to be one of the most important elements in producing a beautiful, well fitting knitted garment. The tension controls the size and shape of your finished piece and any variation to either stitches or rows, however slight, will affect your work and change the fit completely.
To avoid any disappointment, we would always recommend that you knit a tension square in the yarn and stitch given in the pattern, working perhaps four or five more stitches and rows than those given in the tension note. When counting the tension, place your knitting on a flat surface and mark out a 10cm square with pins. Count the stitches between the pins. If you have too many stitches to 10cm your knitting it too tight, try again using thicker needles, if you have too few stitches to 10cm your knitting is too loose, so try again using finer needles. Please note, if you are unable to achieve the correct stitches and rows required, the stitches are more crucial as many patterns are knitted to length.
Keep an eye on your tension during knitting, especially if you're going back to work which has been put to one side for any length of time.

SIZING
The instructions are given for the smallest size. Where they vary, work the figures in brackets for the larger sizes. One set of figures refers to all sizes. The size diagram with each pattern will help you decide which size to knit. The measurements given on the size diagram are the actual size your garment should be when completed.
Measurements will vary from design to design because the necessary ease allowances have been made in each pattern to give your garment the correct fit, i.e. a loose fitting garment will be several cm wider than a neat fitted one, a snug fitting garment may have no ease at all.

WRAP STITCH
A wrap stitch is used to eliminate the hole created when using the short row shaping method. Work to the position on the row indicated in the pattern, wrap the next st (by slipping next st onto right needle, taking yarn to opposite side of work between needles and then slipping same st back onto left needle – on foll rows, K tog the loop and the wrapped st) and turn, cont from pattern.

CHART NOTE
Some of our patterns include a chart. Each square on a chart represent a stitch and each line of squares a row of knitting.
When working from a chart, unless otherwise stated, read odd rows (RS) from right to left and even rows (WS) from left to right. The key alongside each chart indicates how each stitch is worked.

INTARSIA TECHNIQUE
The intarsia method of knitting produces a single thickness of fabric and is used where a colour is only required in a particular area of a row. Use short lengths of yarn for each block of colour, then joining in the different colours at the appropriate point on the row. Ink one colour to the next by twisting them around each other where they meet on the wrong side to avoid gaps. Ends can then be darned along the colour join lines, as each motif is completed.

FAIRISLE TYPE KNITTING
When two or three colours are worked repeatedly across a row, strand the yarn not is use loosely behind the stitches being worked, stretching the stitches to their correct width to keep them elastic.
It is advisable not to carry the stranded or 'floating' yarns over more than three stitches at a time, but to weave them under and over the colour you are working. The 'floating' yarns are therefore caught at the back of the work.

FINISHING INSTRUCTIONS
It is the pressing and finishing which will transform your knitted pieces into a garment to be proud of.
Pressing
Darn in ends neatly along the selvage edge. Follow closely any special instructions given on the pattern or ball band and always take great care not to over press your work.
Block out your knitting on a pressing or ironing board, easing into shape, and unless otherwise states, press each piece using a warm iron over a damp cloth.

Tip: Attention should be given to ribs/edgings; if the garment is close fitting – steam the ribs gently so that the stitches fill out but stay elastic. Alternatively if the garment is to hang straight then steam out to the correct shape.
Tip: Take special care to press the selvages, as this will make sewing up both easier and neater.

CONSTRUCTION
Stitching together
When stitching the pieces together, remember to match areas of pattern very carefully where they meet. Use a stitch such as back stitch or mattress stitch for all main knitting seams and join all ribs and neckband with mattress stitch, unless otherwise stated.
Take extra care when stitching the edgings and collars around the back neck of a garment. They control the width of the back neck, and if too wide the garment will be ill fitting and drop off the shoulder.
Knit back neck edgings only to the length stated in the pattern, even stretching it slightly if for example, you are working in garter or horizontal rib stitch.
Stitch edgings/collars firmly into place using a back stitch seam, easing-in the back neck to fit the collar/edging rather than stretching the collar/edging to fit the back neck.

CARE INSTRUCTIONS

Yarns
Follow the care instructions printed on each individual ball band. Where different yarns are used in the same garment, follow the care instructions for the more delicate one.

Buttons
We recommend that buttons are removed if your garment is to be machine washed.

CROCHET
We are aware that crochet terminology varies from country to country. Please note we have used the English style in this publication.

Crochet abbreviations

ch	chain
ss	slip stitch
dc	double crochet
tr	treble
dc2tog	2 dc tog
tr2tog	2 tr tog
yoh	yarn over hook

Double crochet
1. Insert the hook into the work (as indicated in the pattern), wrap the yarn over the hook and draw the yarn through the work only.
2. Wrap the yarn again and draw the yarn through both loops on the hook.
3. 1 dc made

Treble
1. Wrap the yarn over the hook and insert the hook into the work (as indicated on the pattern).
2. Wrap the yarn over the hook draw through the work only and wrap the yarn again.
3. Draw through the first 2 loops only and wrap the yarn again.
4. Draw through the last 2 loops on the hook.
5. 1 treble made.

ABBREVIATIONS

K	knit
P	purl
K1b	knit 1 through back loop
st(s)	stitch(es)
inc	increas(e)(ing)
dec	decreas(e)(ing)
st st	stocking stitch (1 row K, 1 row P)
garter st	garter stitch (K every row)
beg	begin(ning)
foll	following
rem	remain(ing)
rev st st	reverse stocking stitch (1 row P, 1 row K)
rep	repeat
alt	alternate
cont	continue
patt	pattern
tog	together
mm	millimetres
cm	centimetres
in(s)	inch(es)
RS	right side
WS	wrong side
sl 1	slip one stitch
psso	pass slipped stitch over
tbl	through back of loop
M1	make one stitch by picking up horizontal loop before next stitch and knitting into back of it
M1p	make one stitch by picking up horizontal loop before next stitch and purling into back of it
yfwd	yarn forward (making a stitch)
yon	yarn over needle (making a stitch)
yrn	yarn round needle (making a stitch)-
MP	Make picot: Cast on 1 st, by inserting the right needle between the first and second stitch on left needle, take yarn round needle, bring loop through and place on left (one stitch cast on), cast off 1 st, by knitting first the loop and then the next stitch, pass the first stitch over the second (one stitch cast off).
Cn	cable needle
C4B	Cable 4 back: Slip next 2 sts onto a cn and hold at back of work, K2, K2 from cn.
C4F	Cable 4 front: Slip next 2 sts onto a cn and hold at front of work, K2, K2 from cn.

100

INDEX

DESIGN	PICTURE	PATTERN
ALANNA	52 & 53	93
ANNIS	18 & 19	70
BLAIR	34 & 35	84
BRAM	22, 32 & 54	76
BRYN	48, 49 & 51	94
CARIS	46 & 47	96
DREW	30 & 31	82
ECHO	7, 8 & 9	58
FARA	28 & 29	80
FOGGY	33	95
ISOLDE	36 & 37	69
MYRA	39, 40 & 41	86
RIPLEY	54, 55 & 57	91
SHALE	10 & 11	61
SMOKY	12, 15 & 38	63
STOMP	20 & 21	72
TEMPEST	12, 13 & 15	64
THOR	24, 25 & 27	77
TYNE	42, 43 & 45	88
WEALD	16 & 17	66
WILDA	22 & 23	74
INFORMATION		98

THANK YOU!

We would like to say a big, big thank you to the fantastic people who have contributed to making this book possible; Graham for the most brilliant photography and editorial design, Angela for her skills on the page layouts, the gorgeous Angharad for making the clothes look incredible, Diana who created the great hair and make-up, as always - Sue and Tricia for their pattern writing & checking expertise, Ella, Sandra, Glennis, Betty, Margaret, Sarah and Joan for all their amazing knitting, Susan for her patience in finishing the garments, Kate, David, Ann and Vicky at Rowan for their support, all at T.K.F. Training www.tkftraining.co.uk, for the fantastic location and finally Jackie for her invaluable last minute help on the shoot.

Kim, Kathleen and Lindsay